Thank you for your purchase!

Color Your Happiness is a coloring book with **Words of Affirmation** to help you practice and believe in the power of **self-love**. The 75 coloring pages are a beautiful combination of mandalas and flowers.

Start your day and end your night with **Words of Affirmation**, such as:
- I am beautiful.
- I am worthy of love.
- My life is abundantly blessed
- I am protected by God's love

Sooner than later, you will witness that your thoughts will **manifest** positive energy, love, opportunities, and happiness.

I HAVE POWER

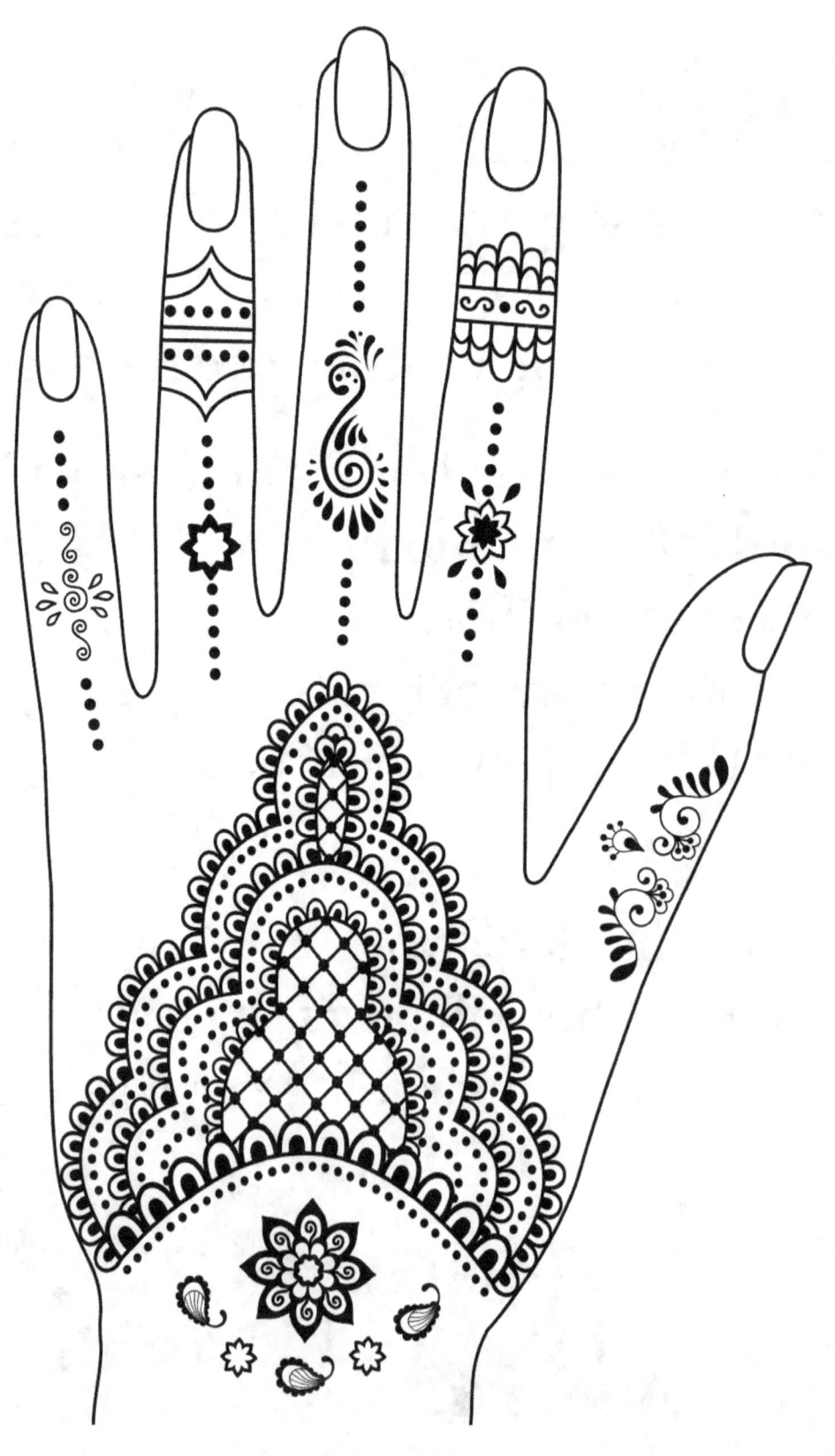

MY FUTURE IS BRIGHT

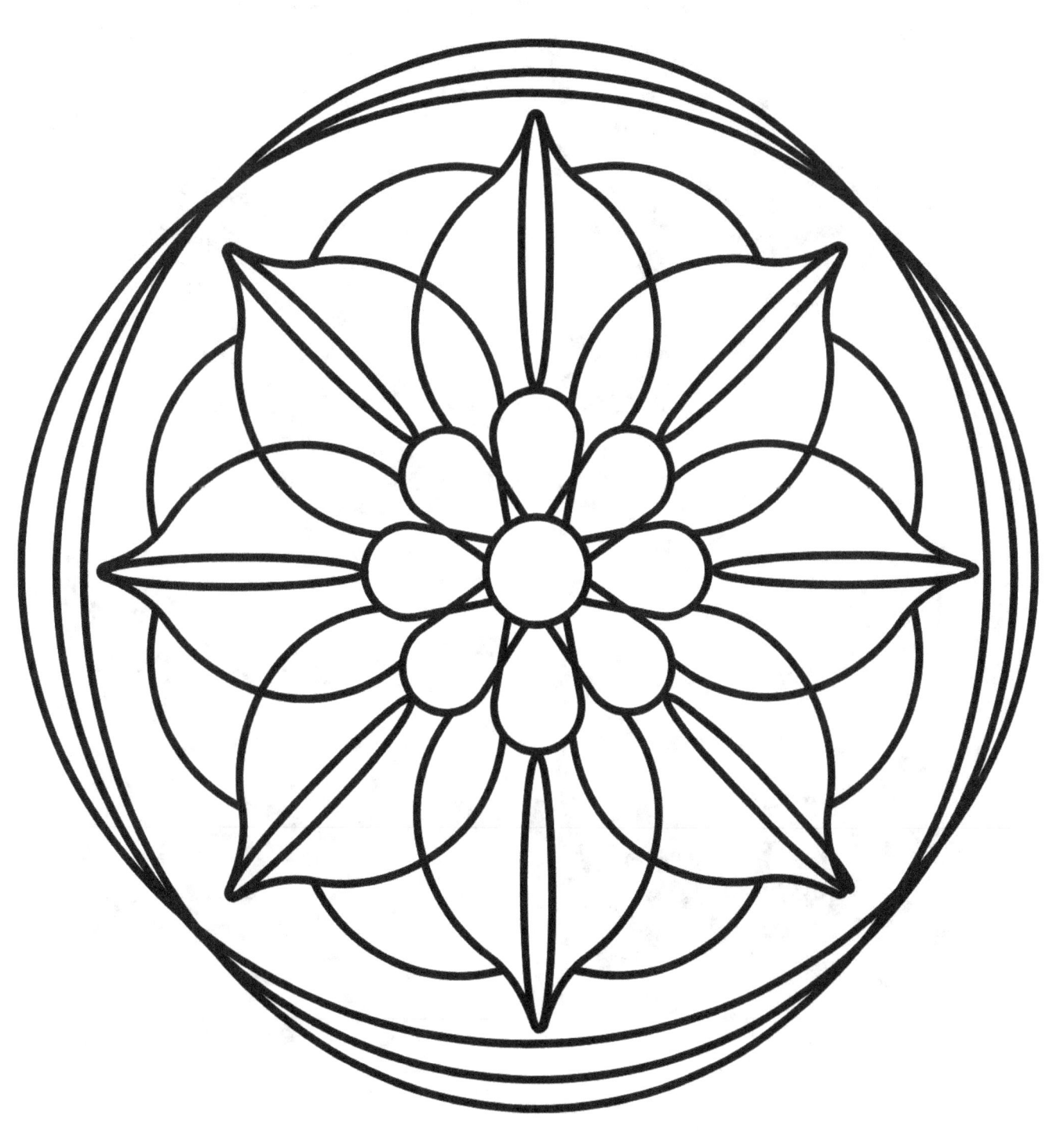

I MATTER

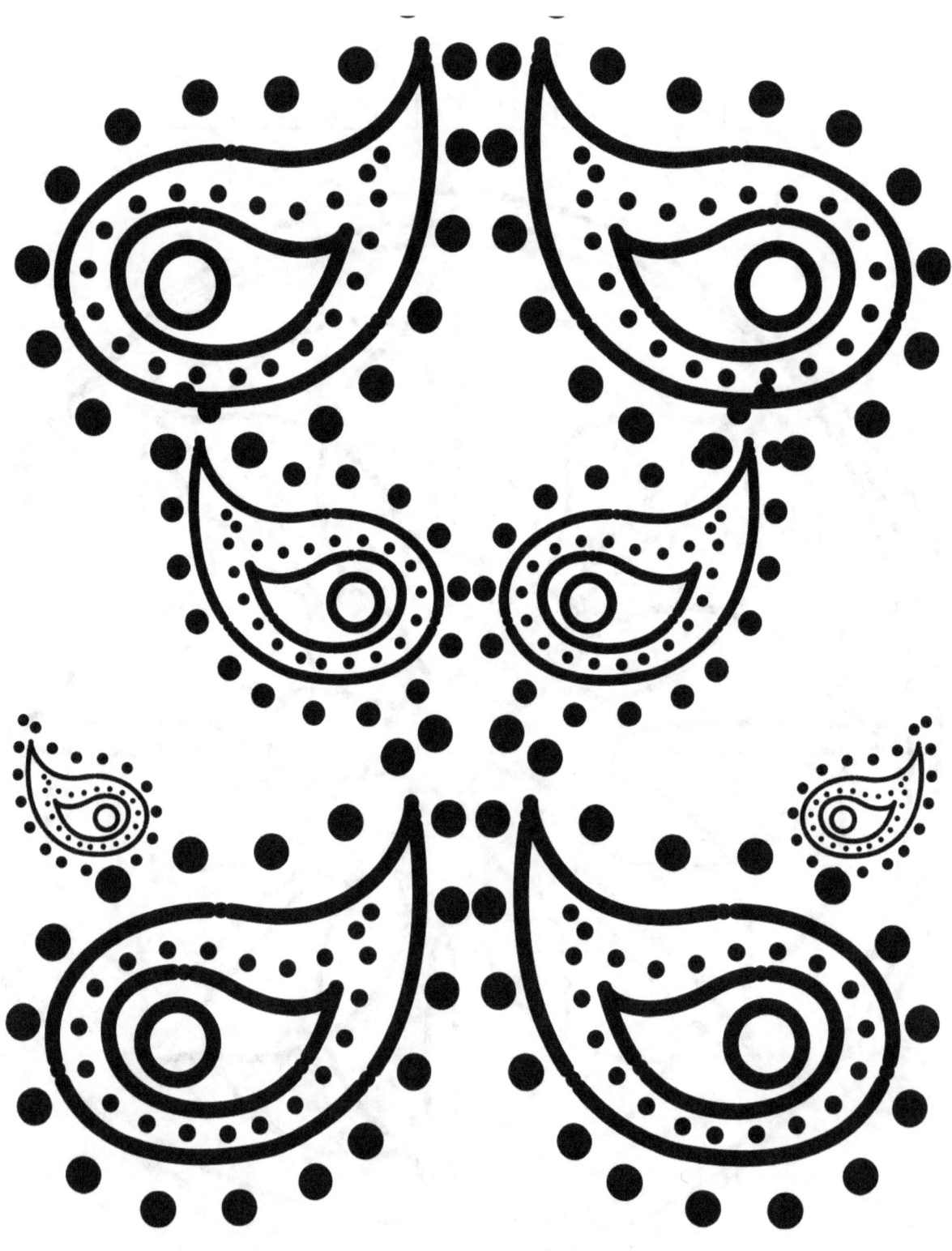

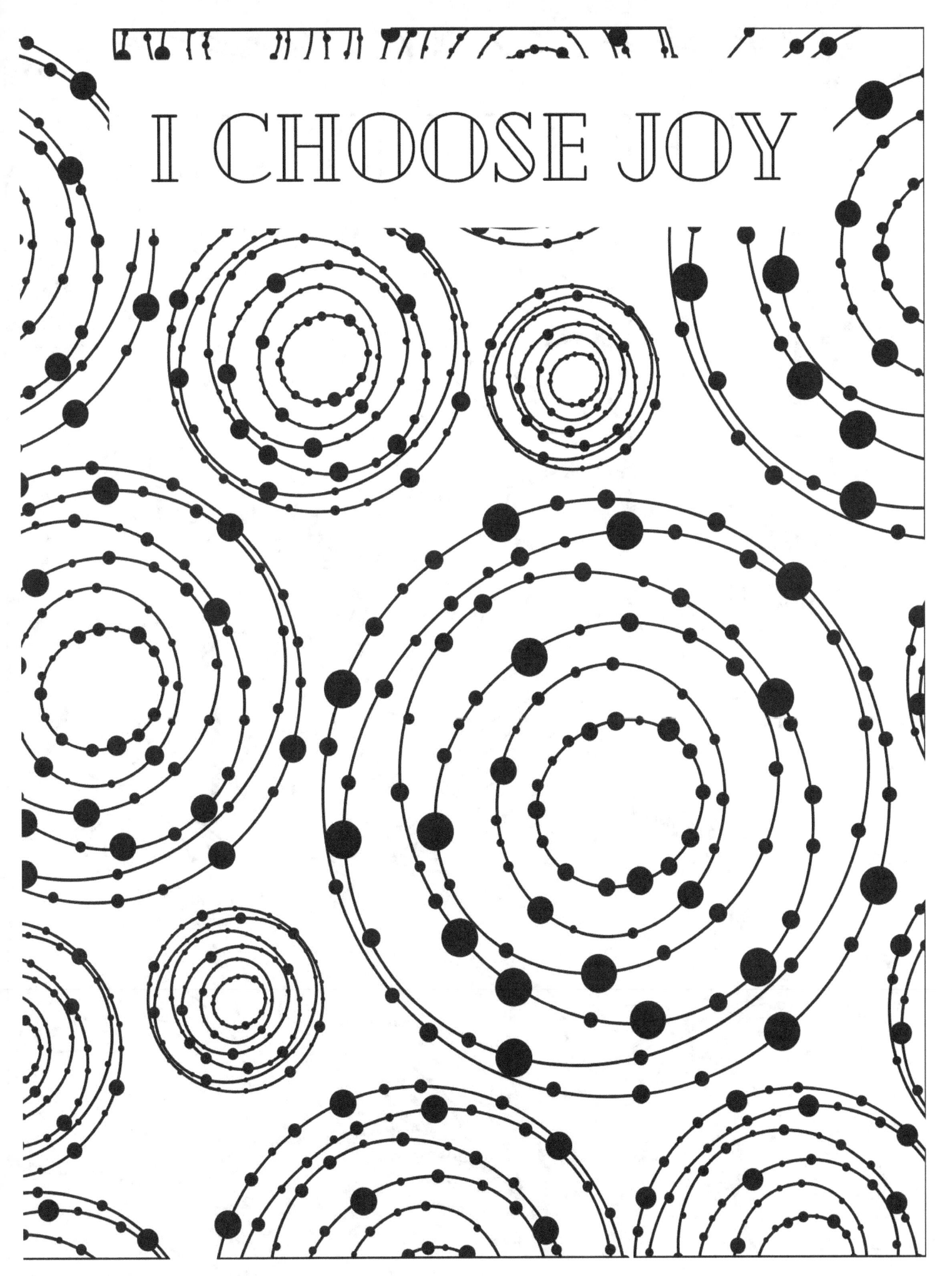

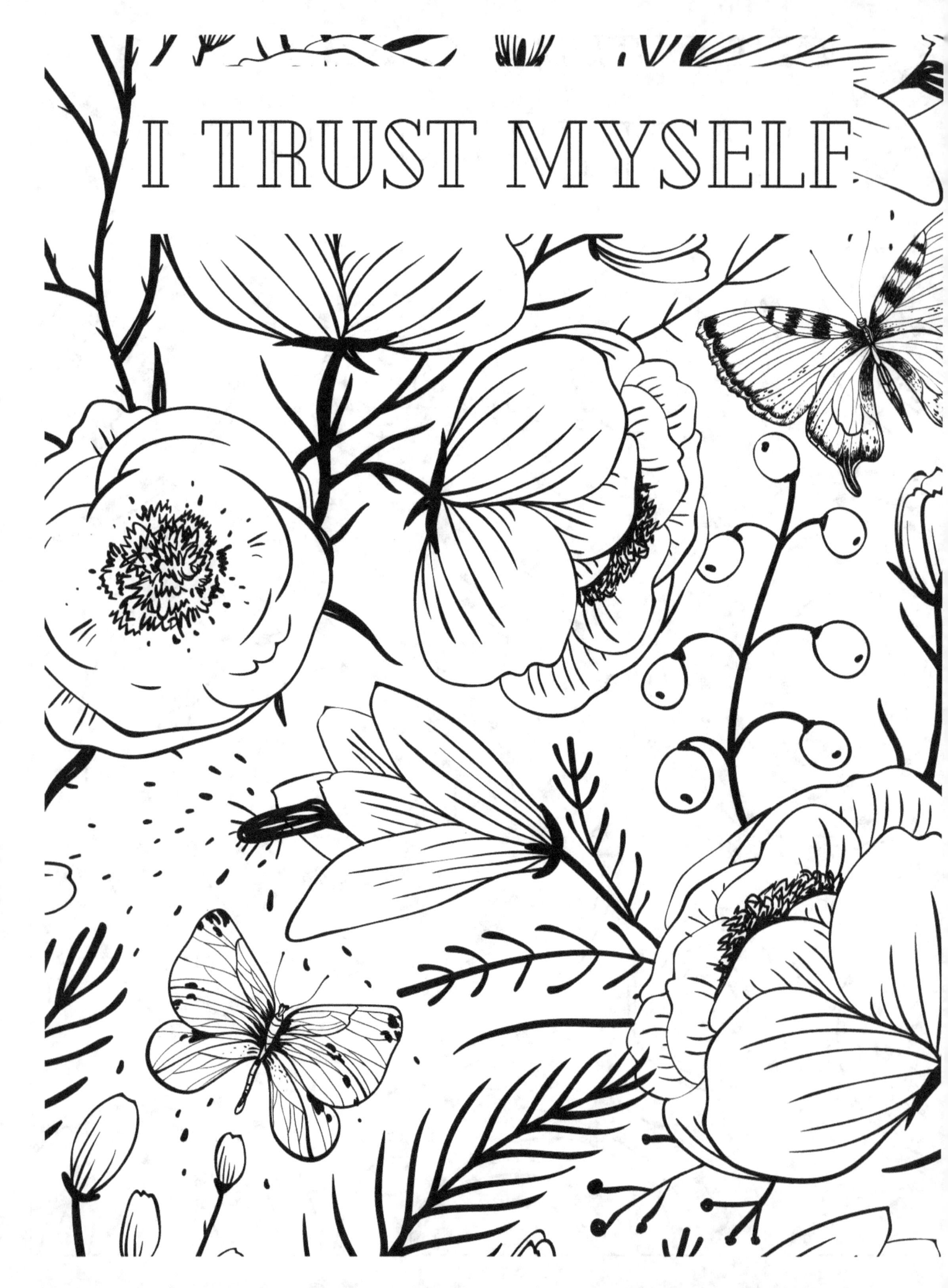

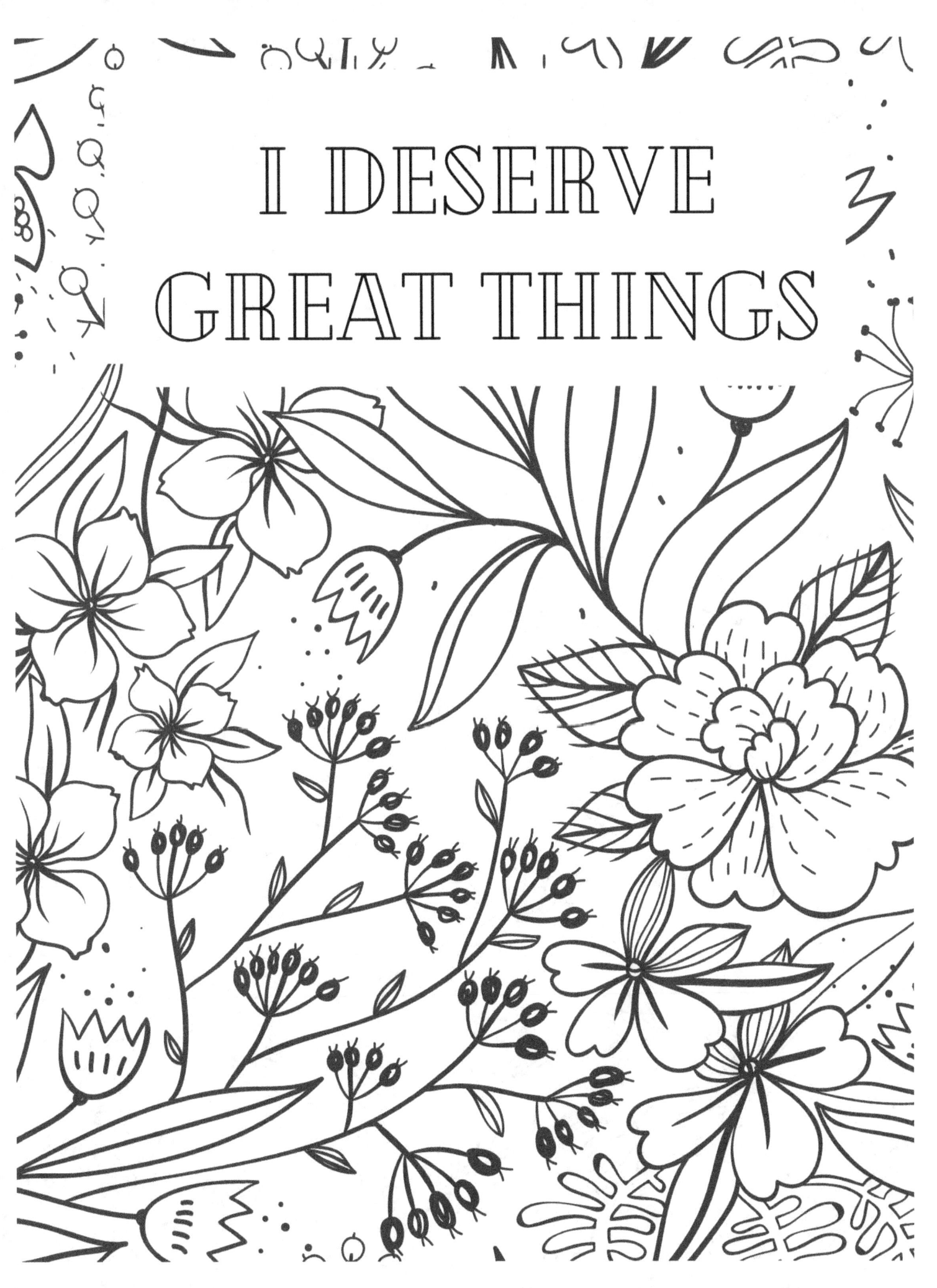

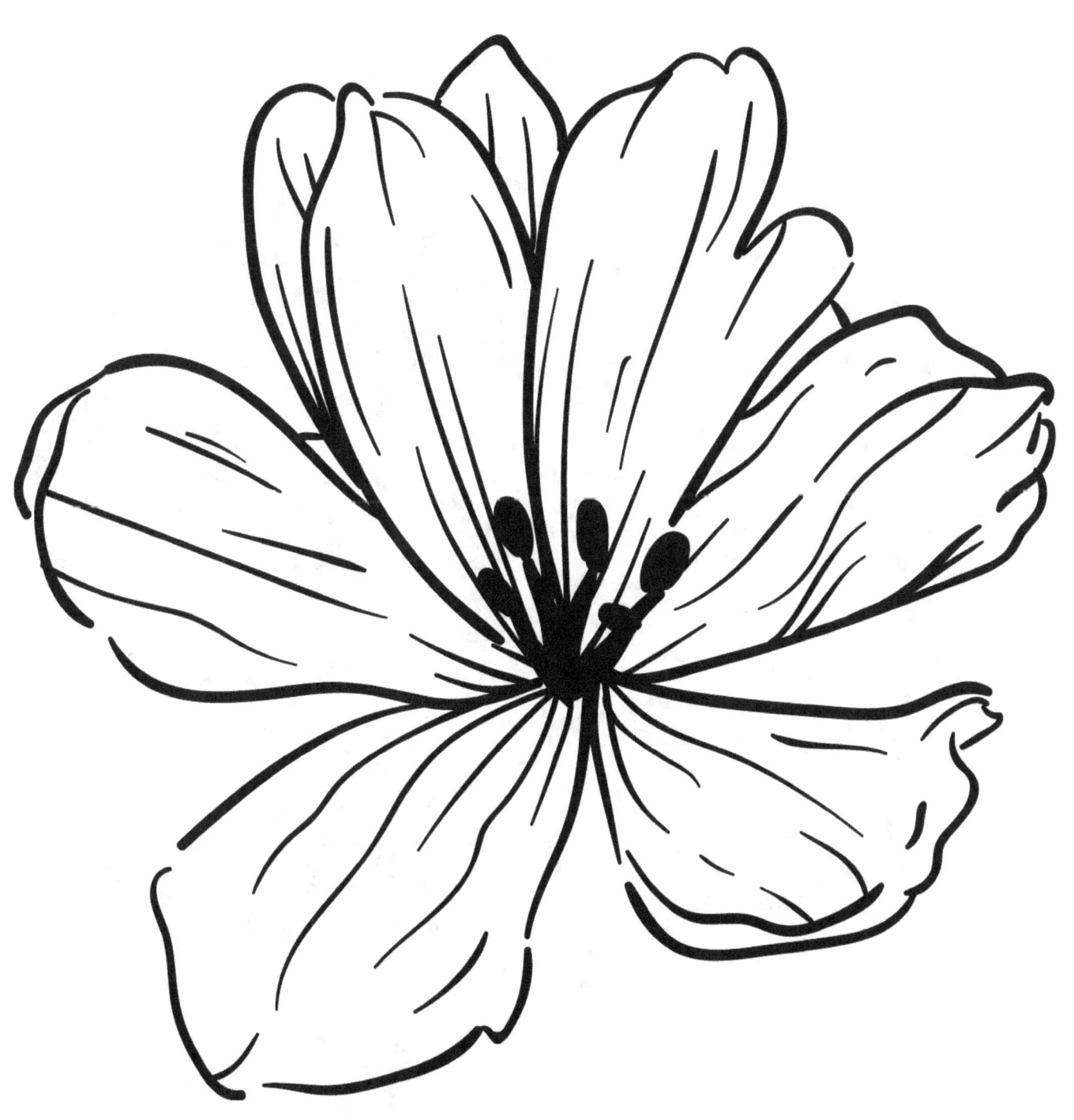

I AM DOING MY BEST!

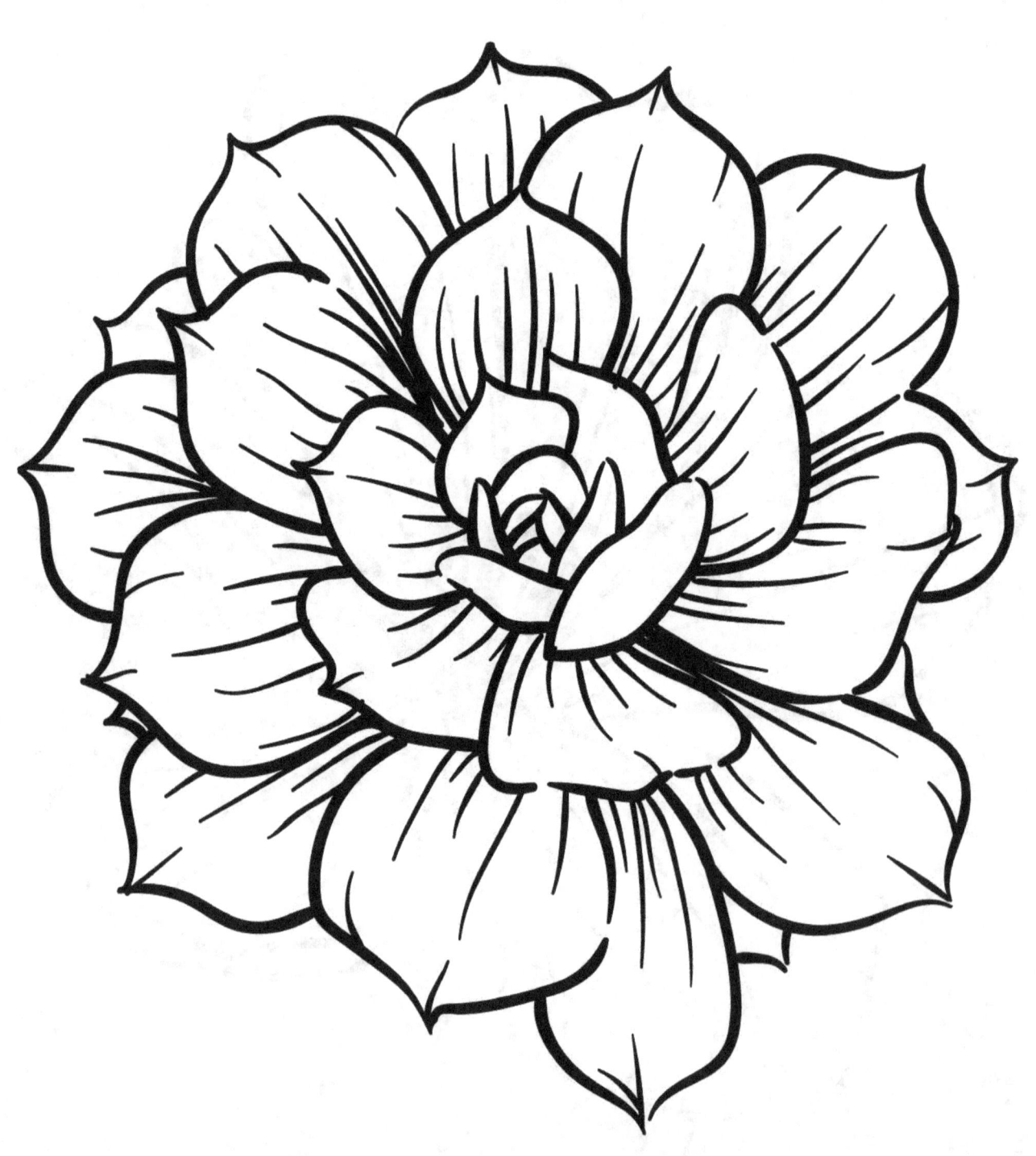

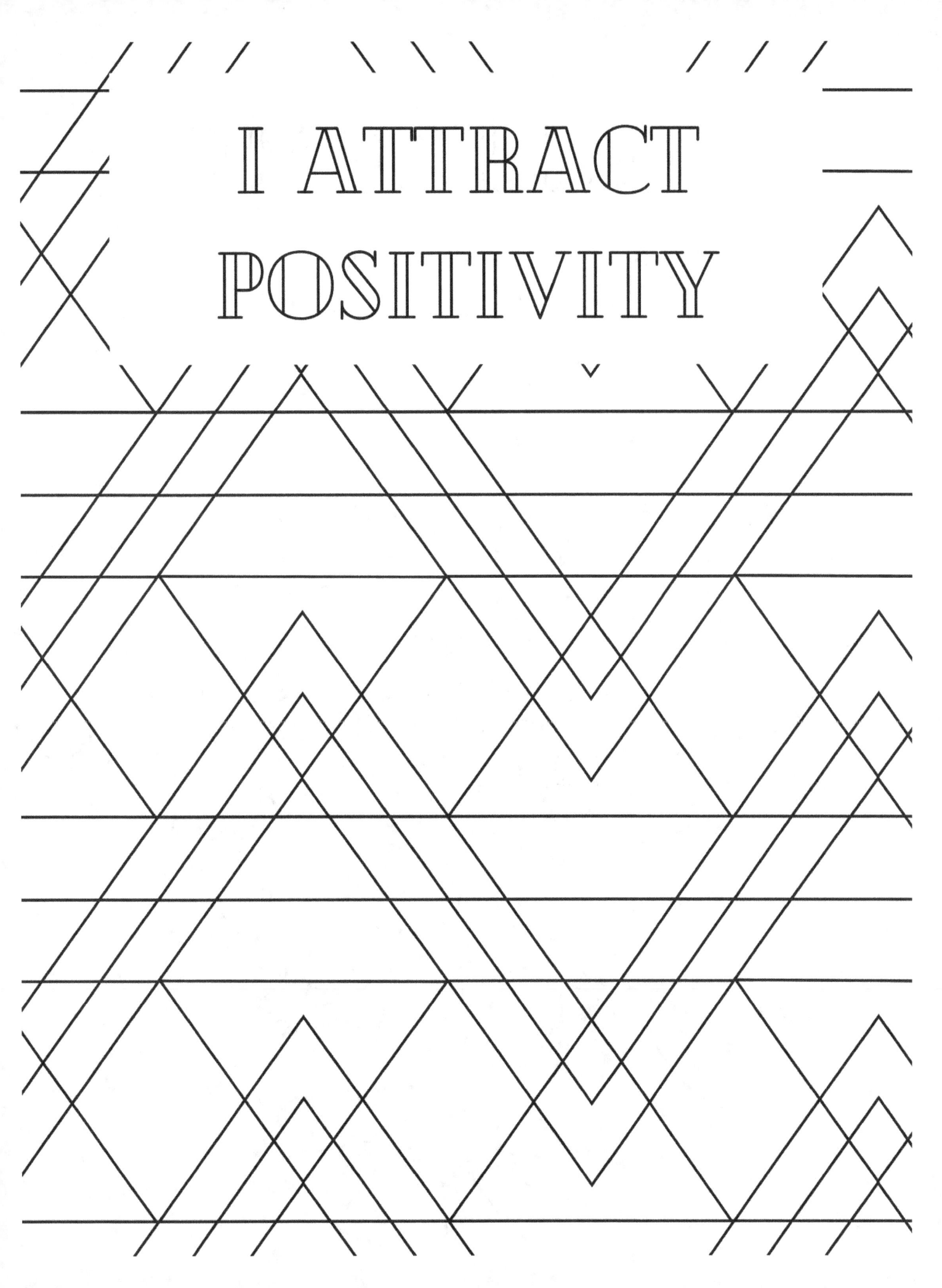

I WELCOME OPPORTUNITIES

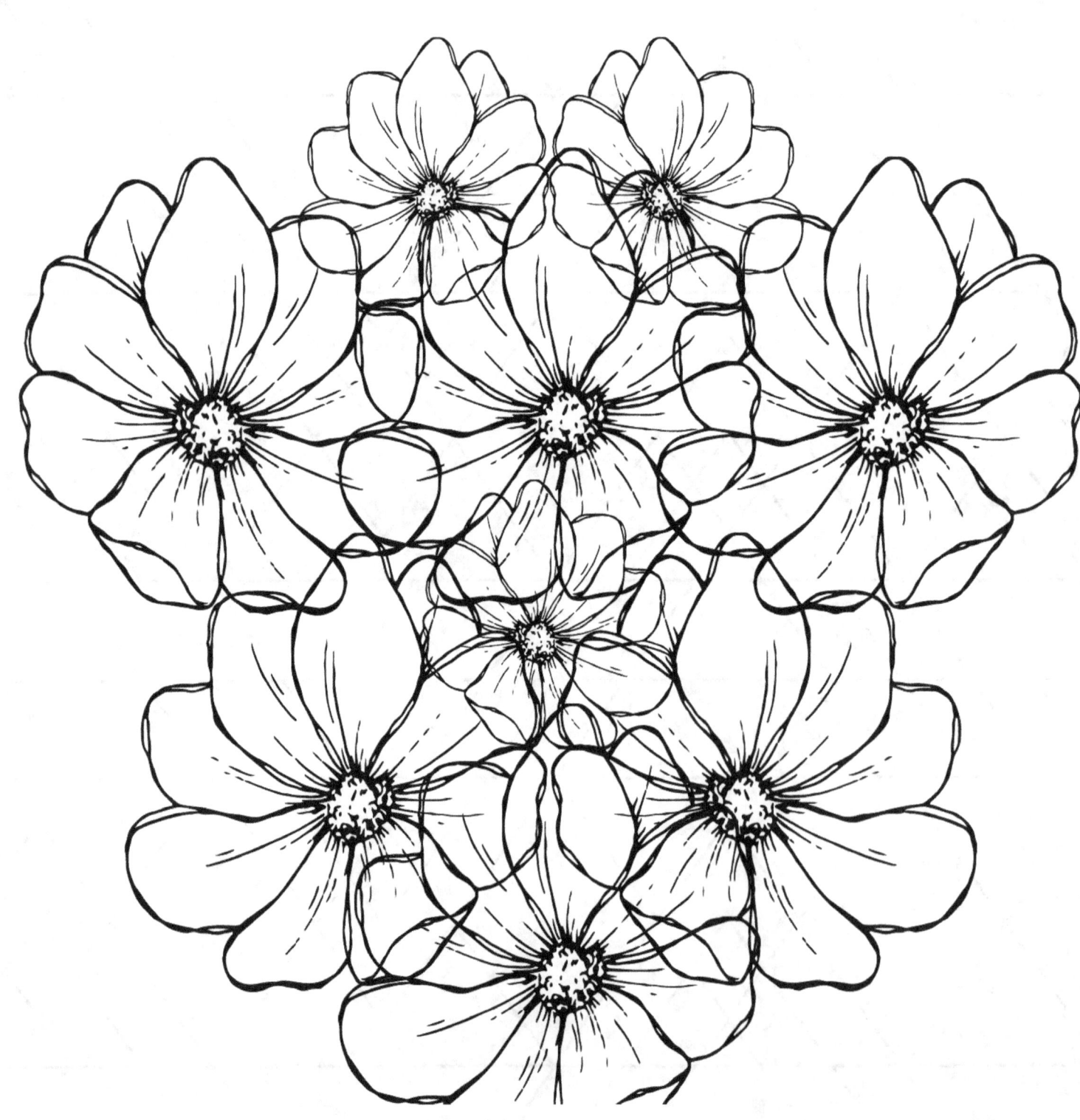

I'M IN MY SEASON

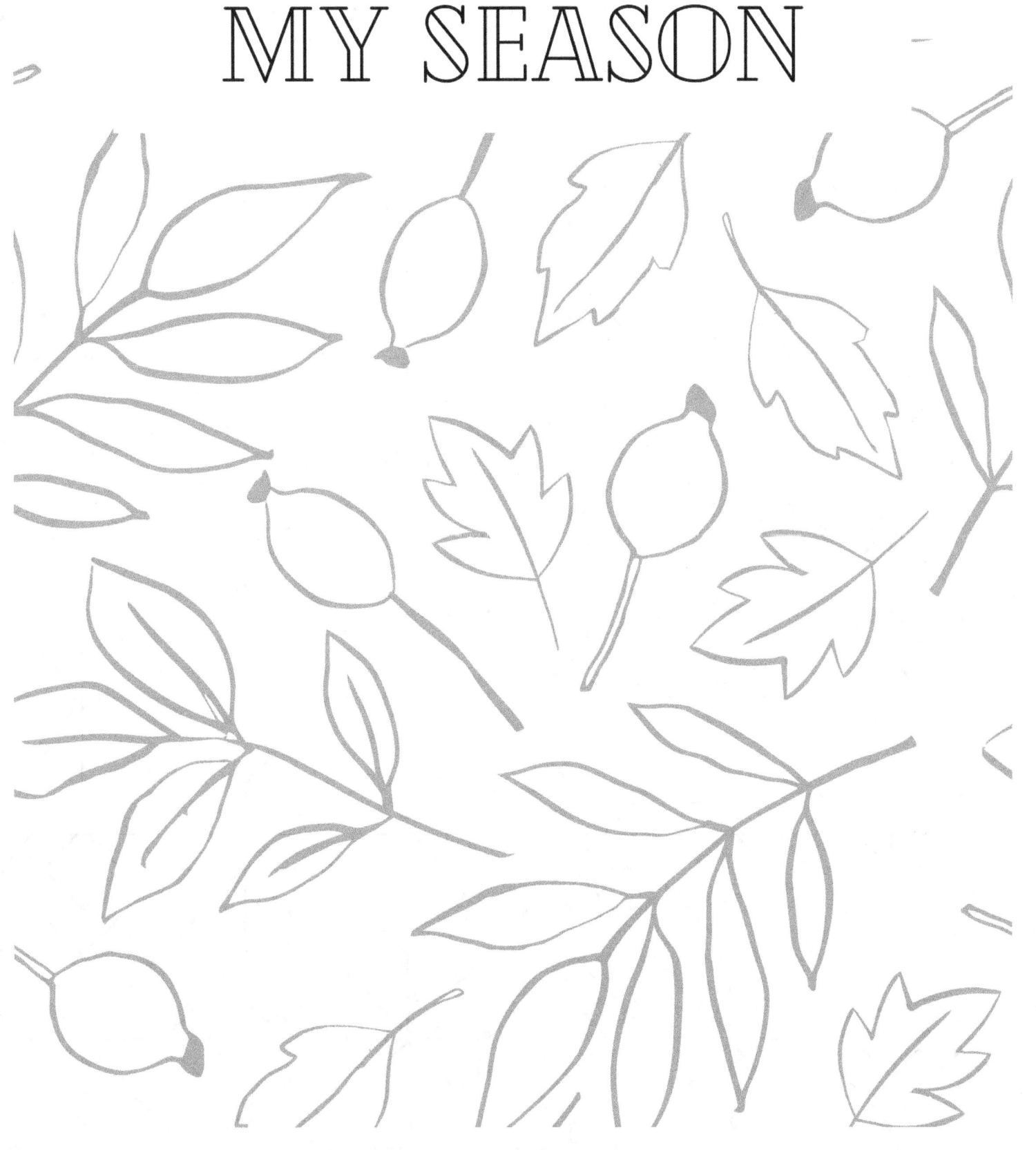

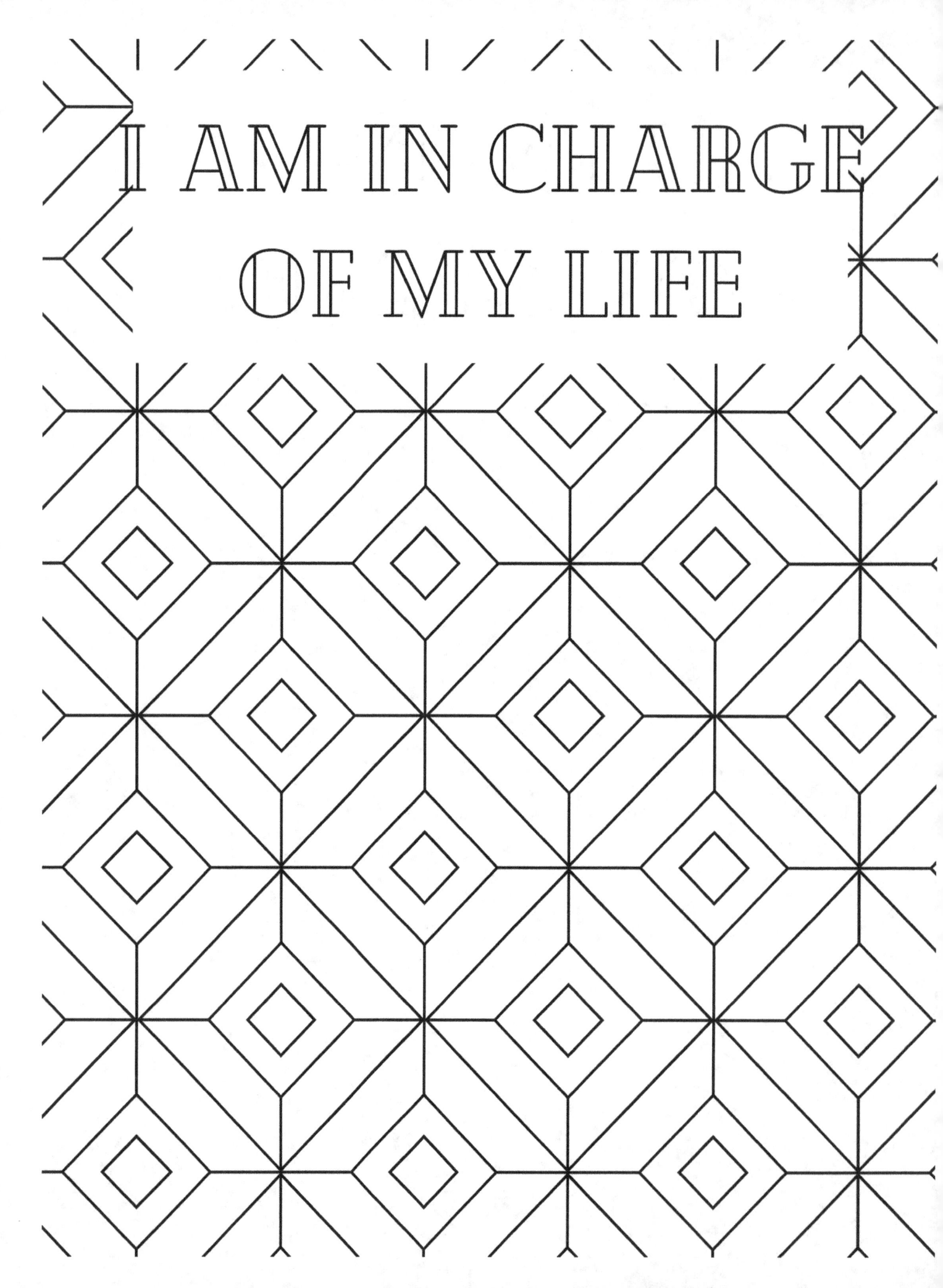

I BELIEVE IN MYSELF

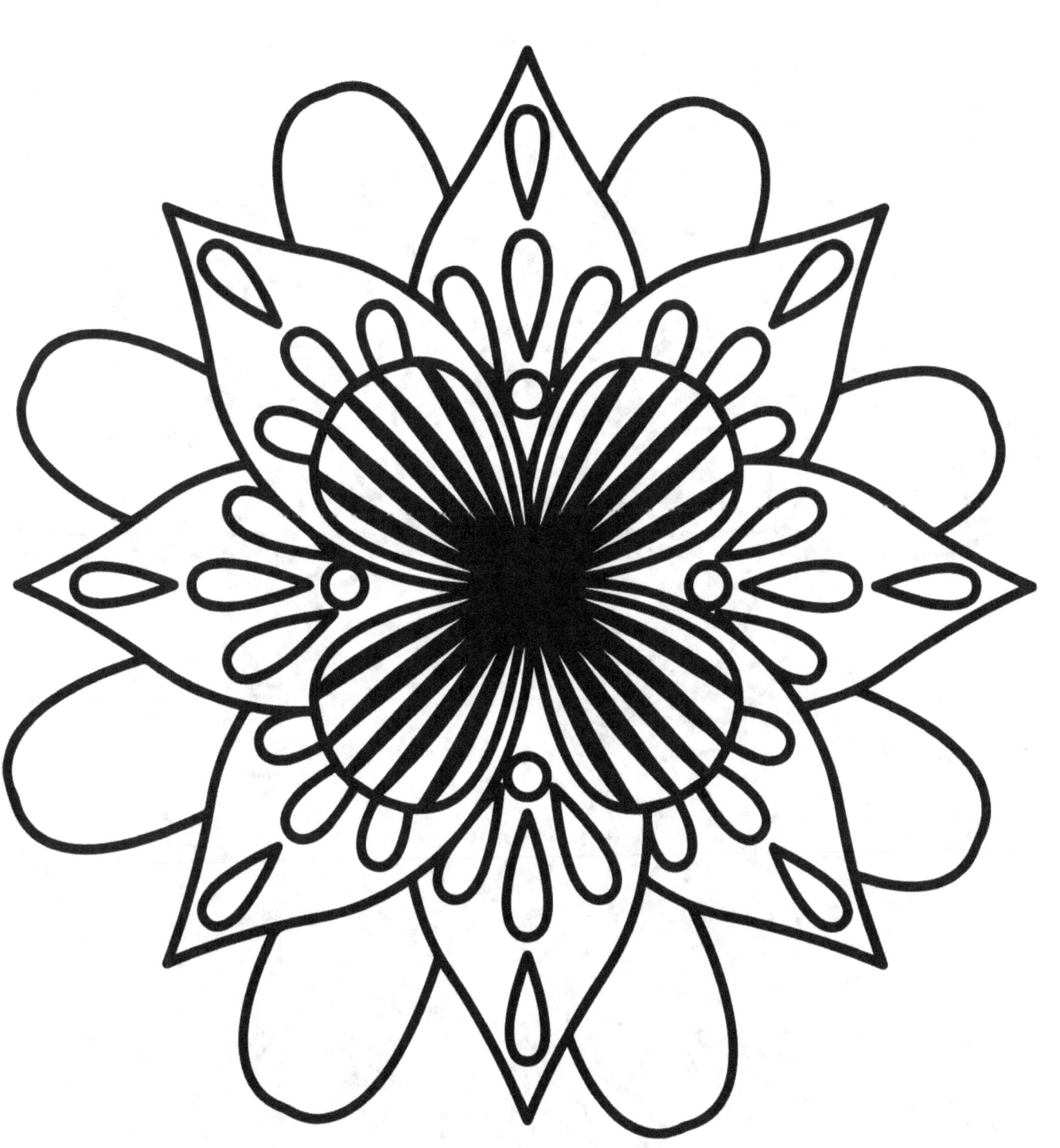

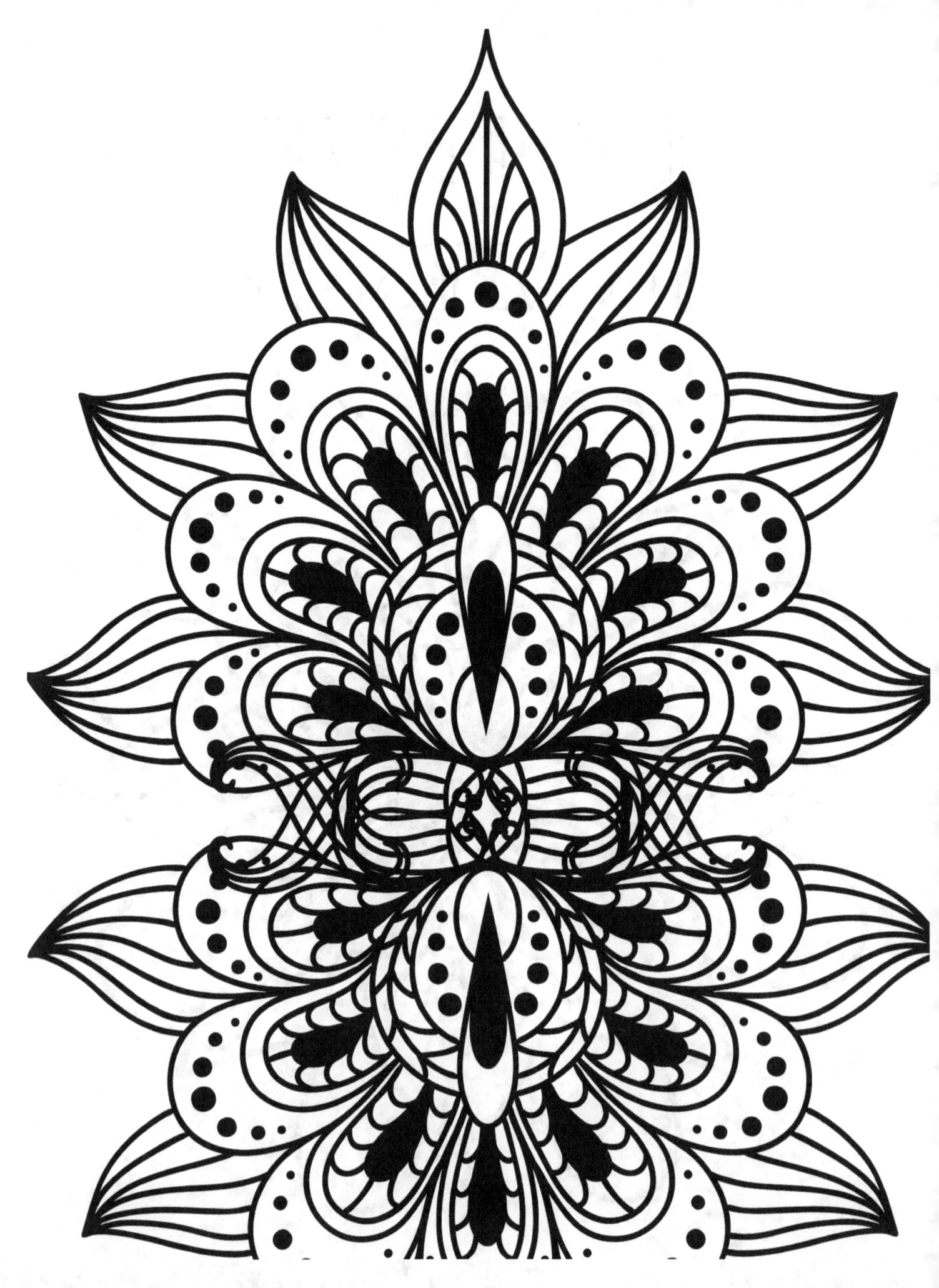

I MAKE MYSELF A PRIORITY

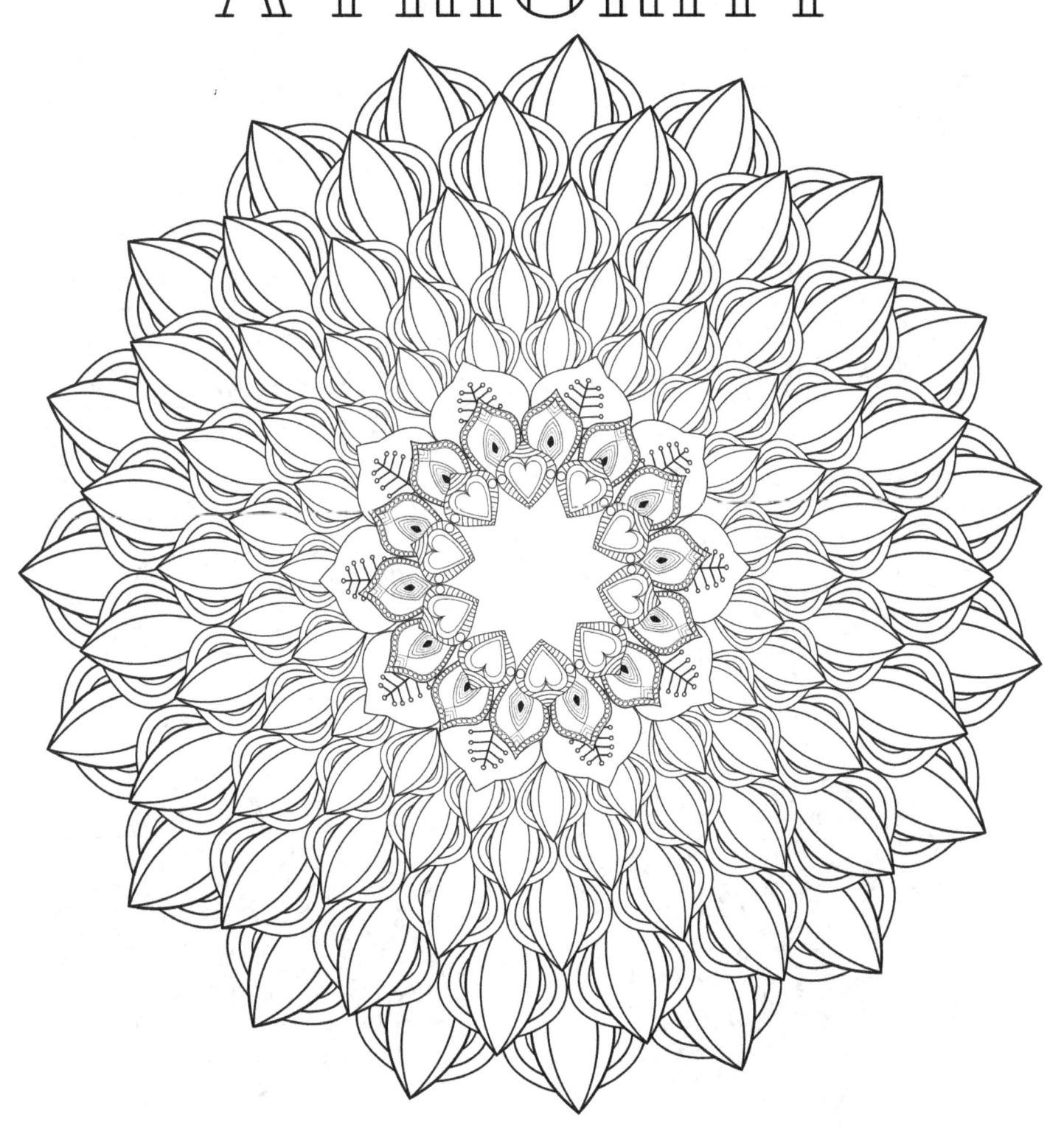

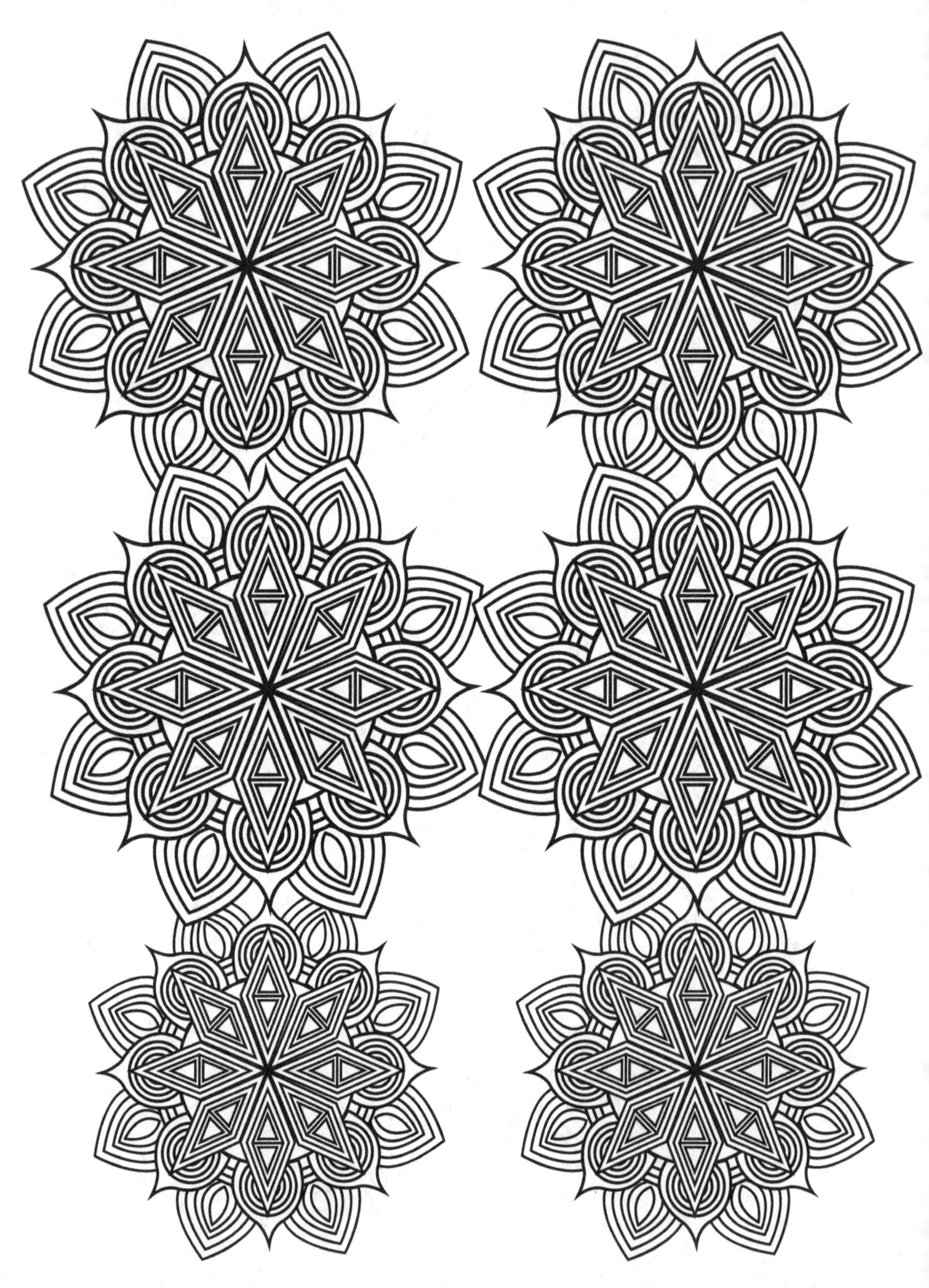

I WILL INVEST IN MYSELF

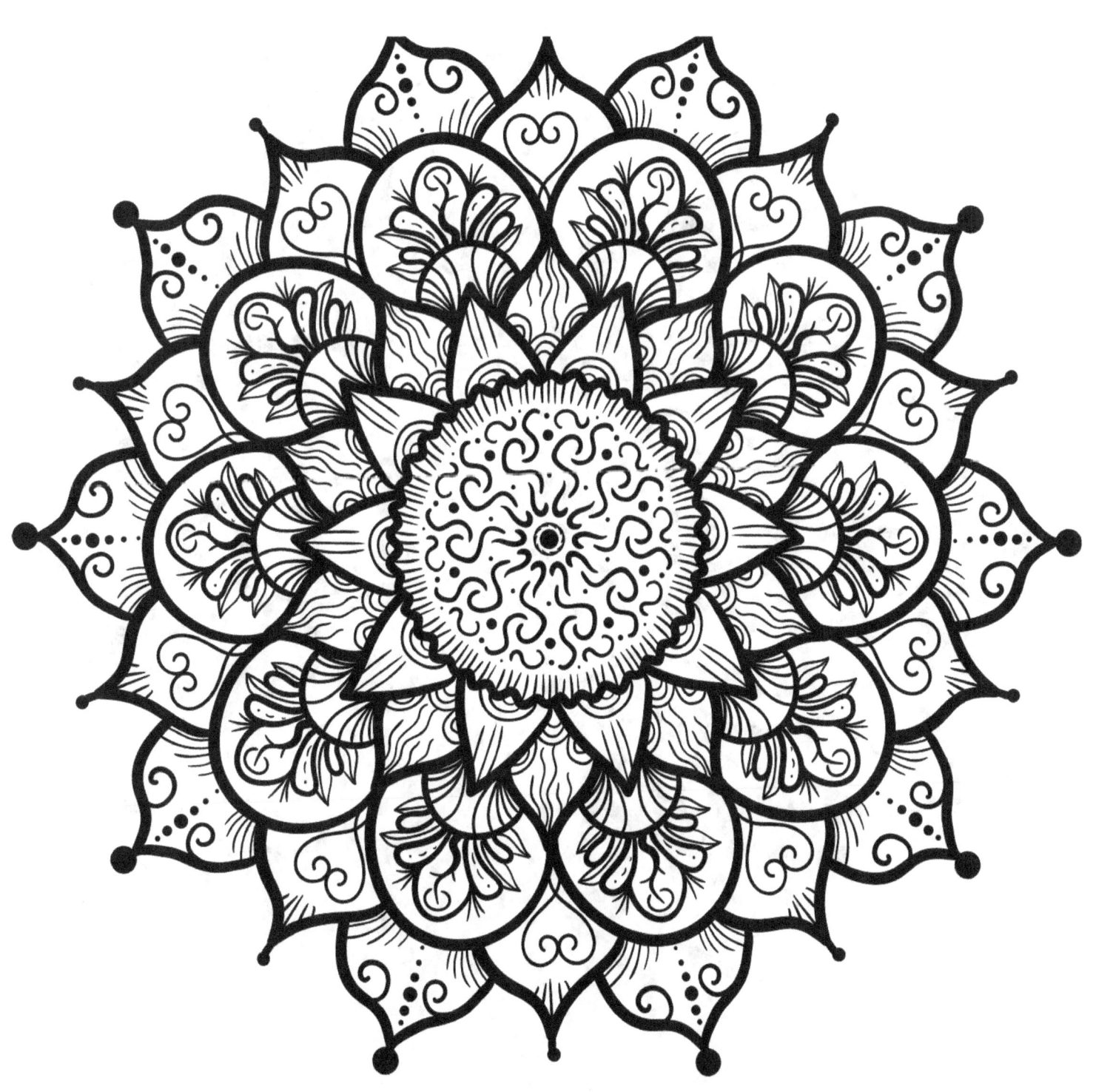

MY CONFIDENCE IS BEAUTIFUL

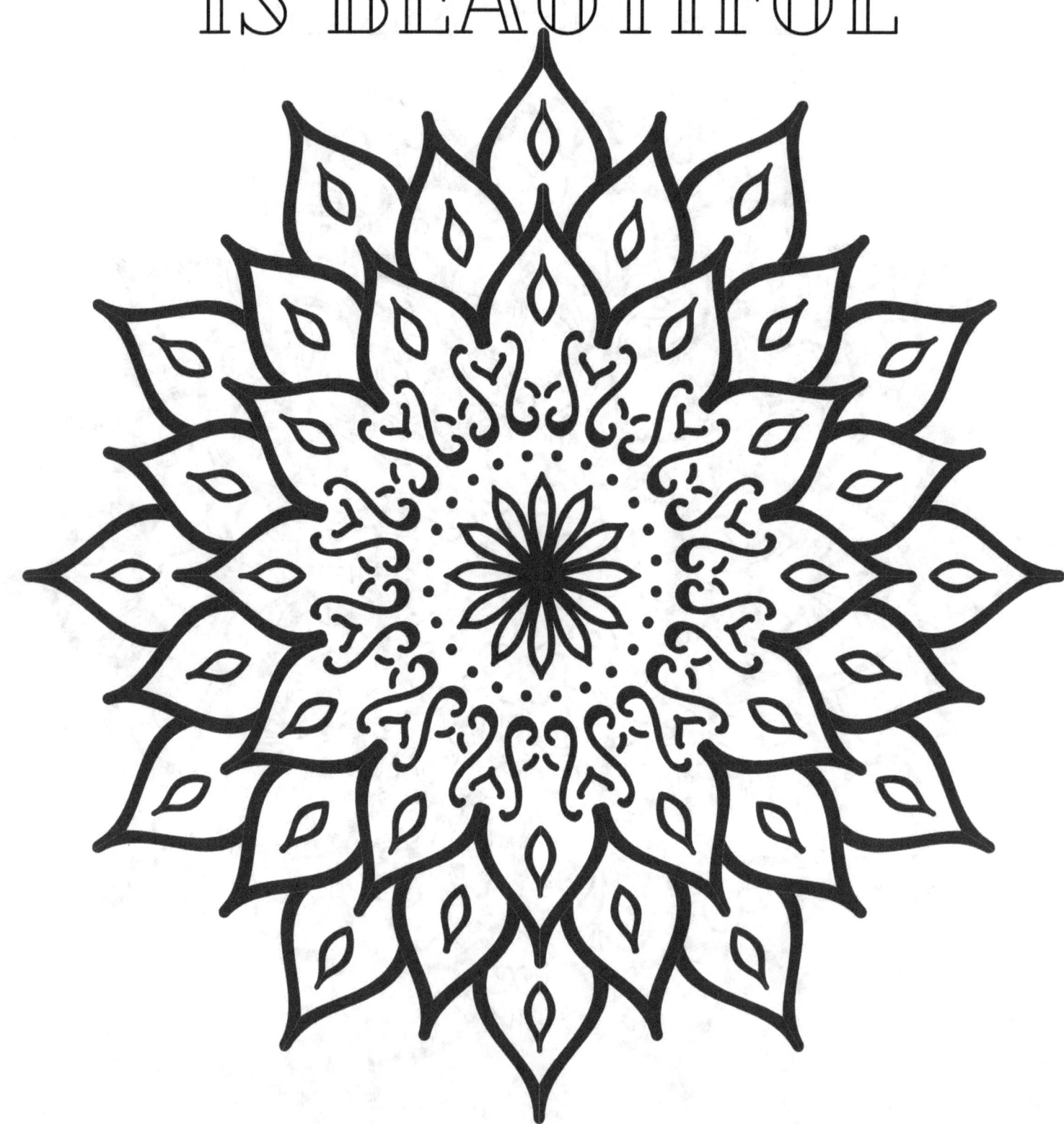

I WILL ACHIEVE MY GOALS

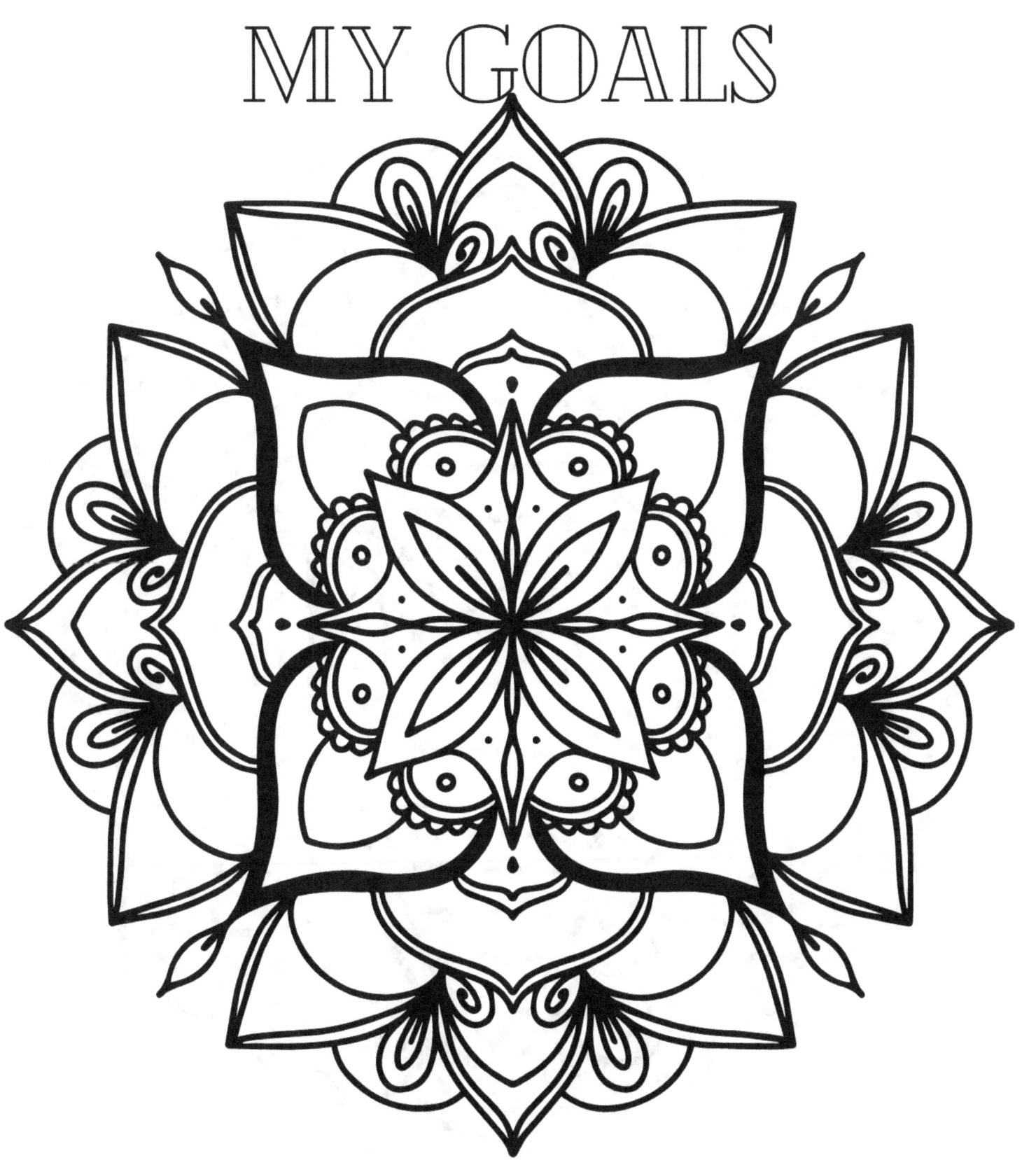

CHANGE IS INEVITABLE

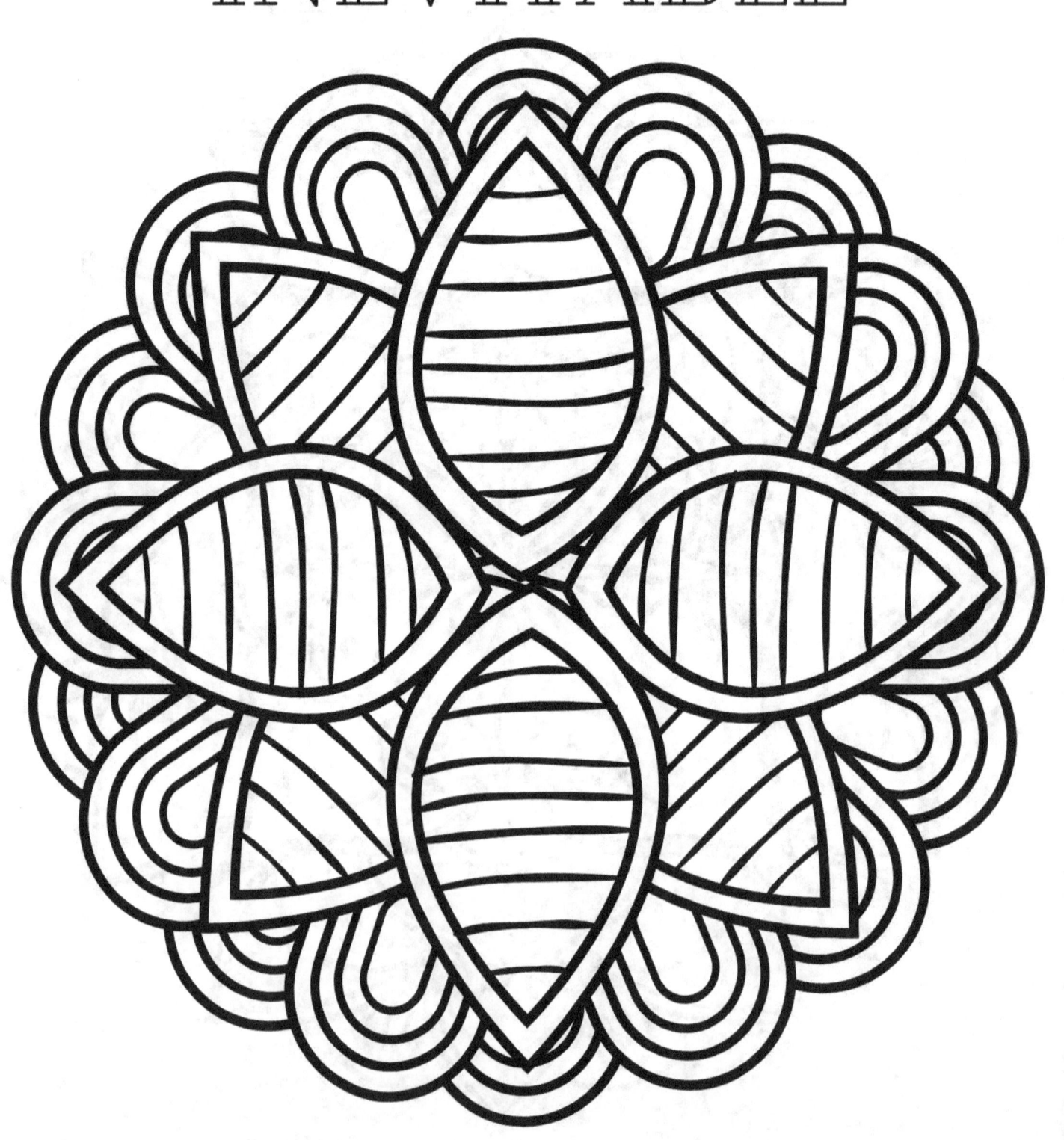

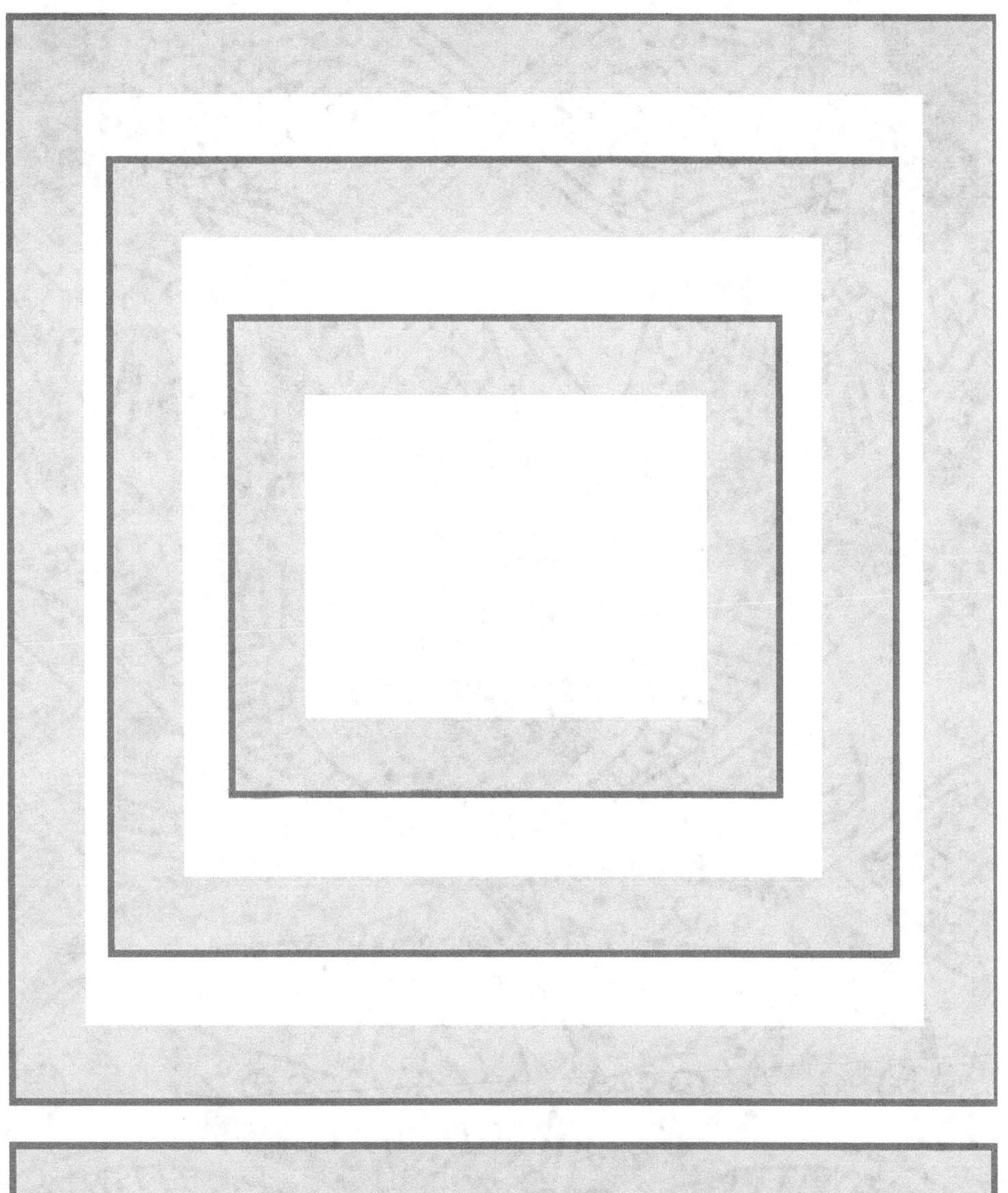

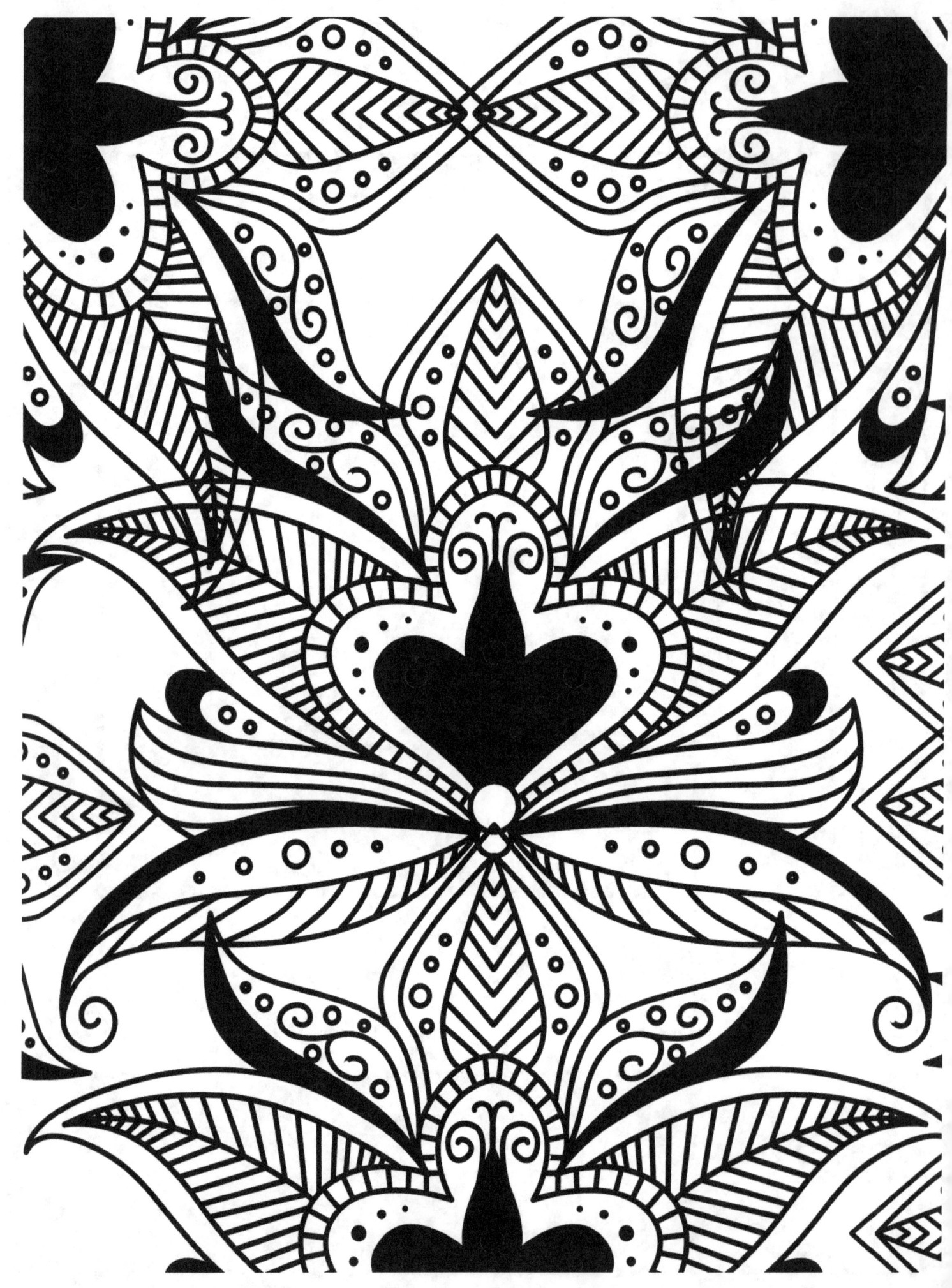

I AM ENOUGH

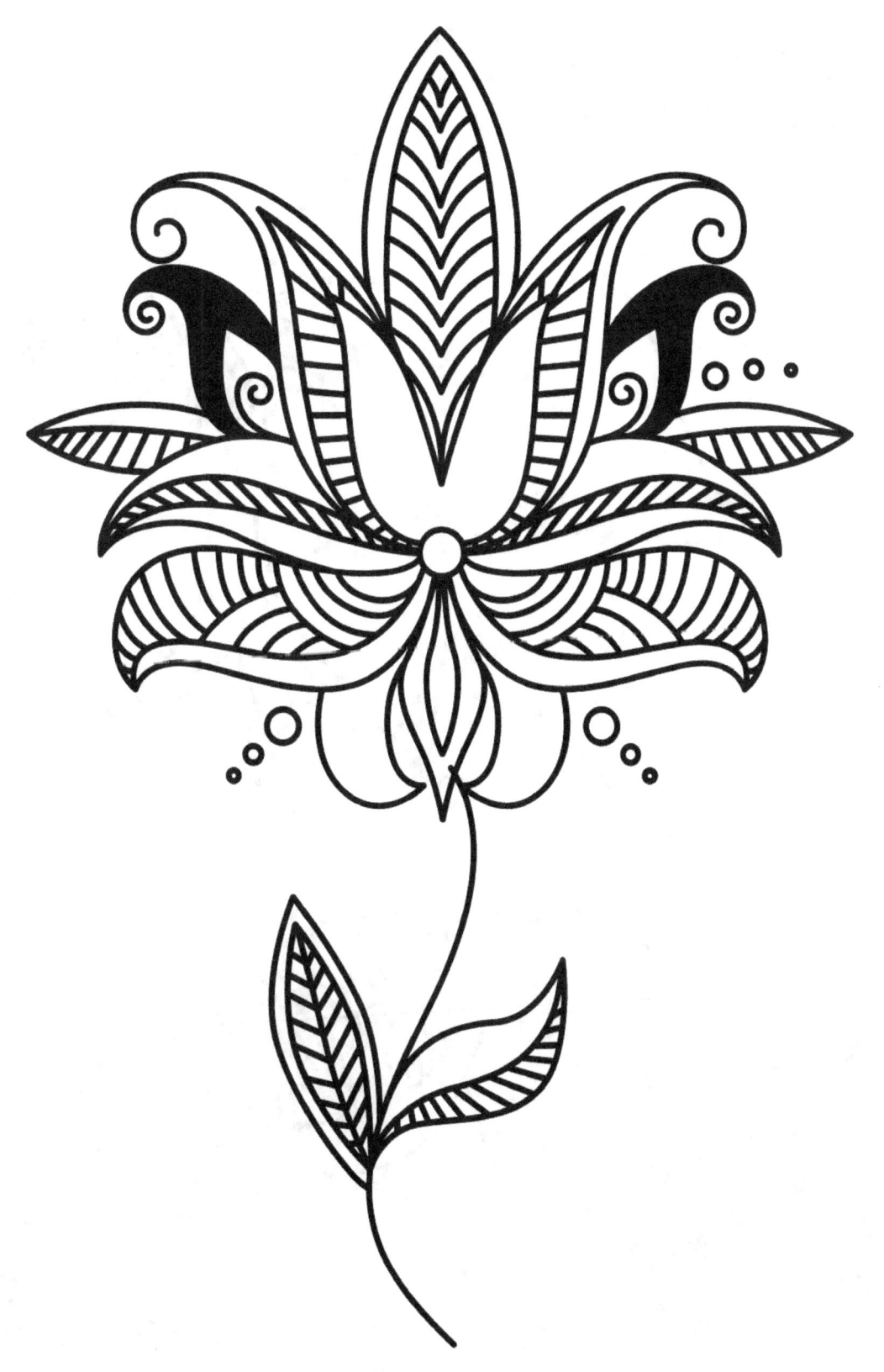

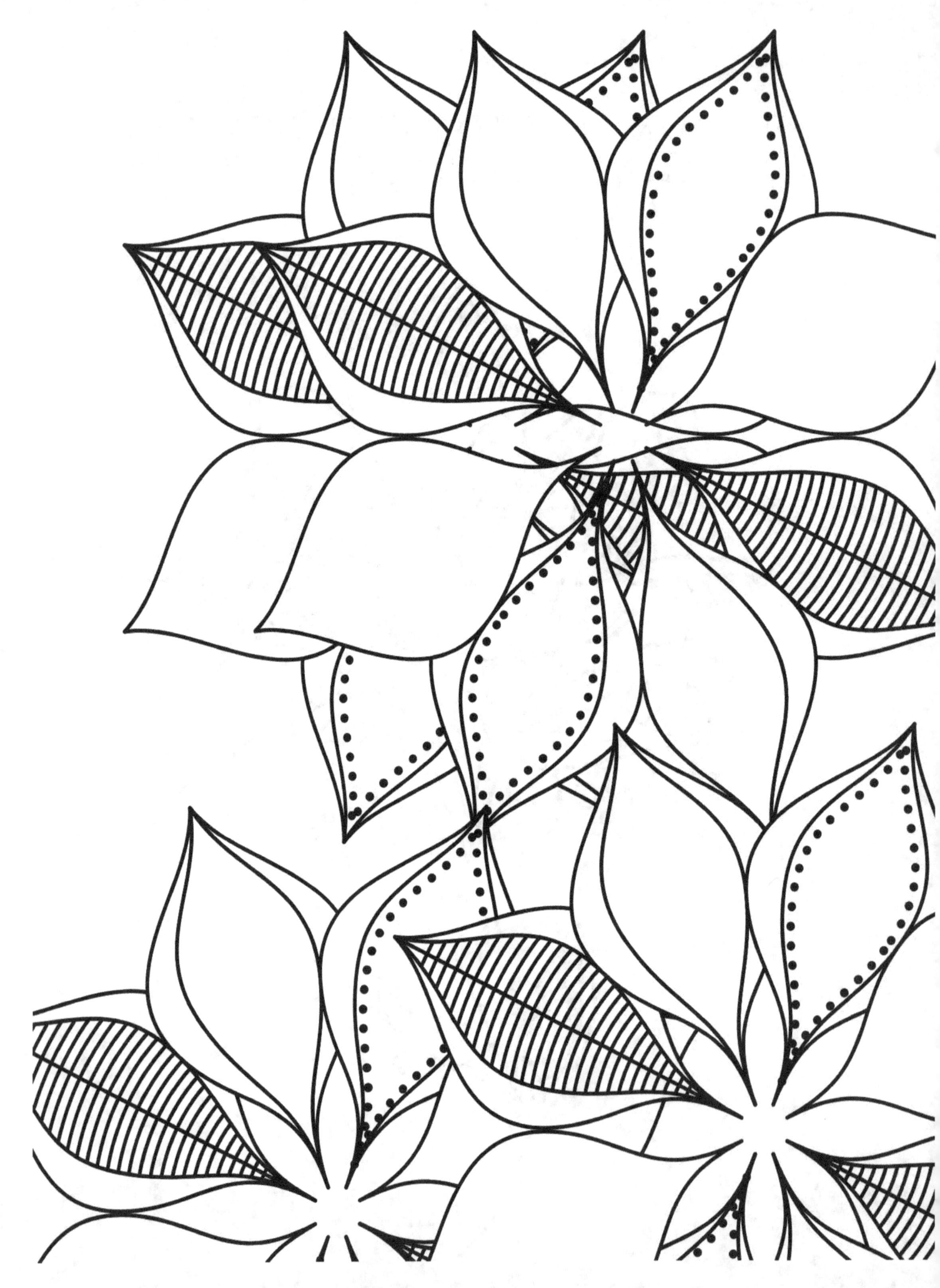

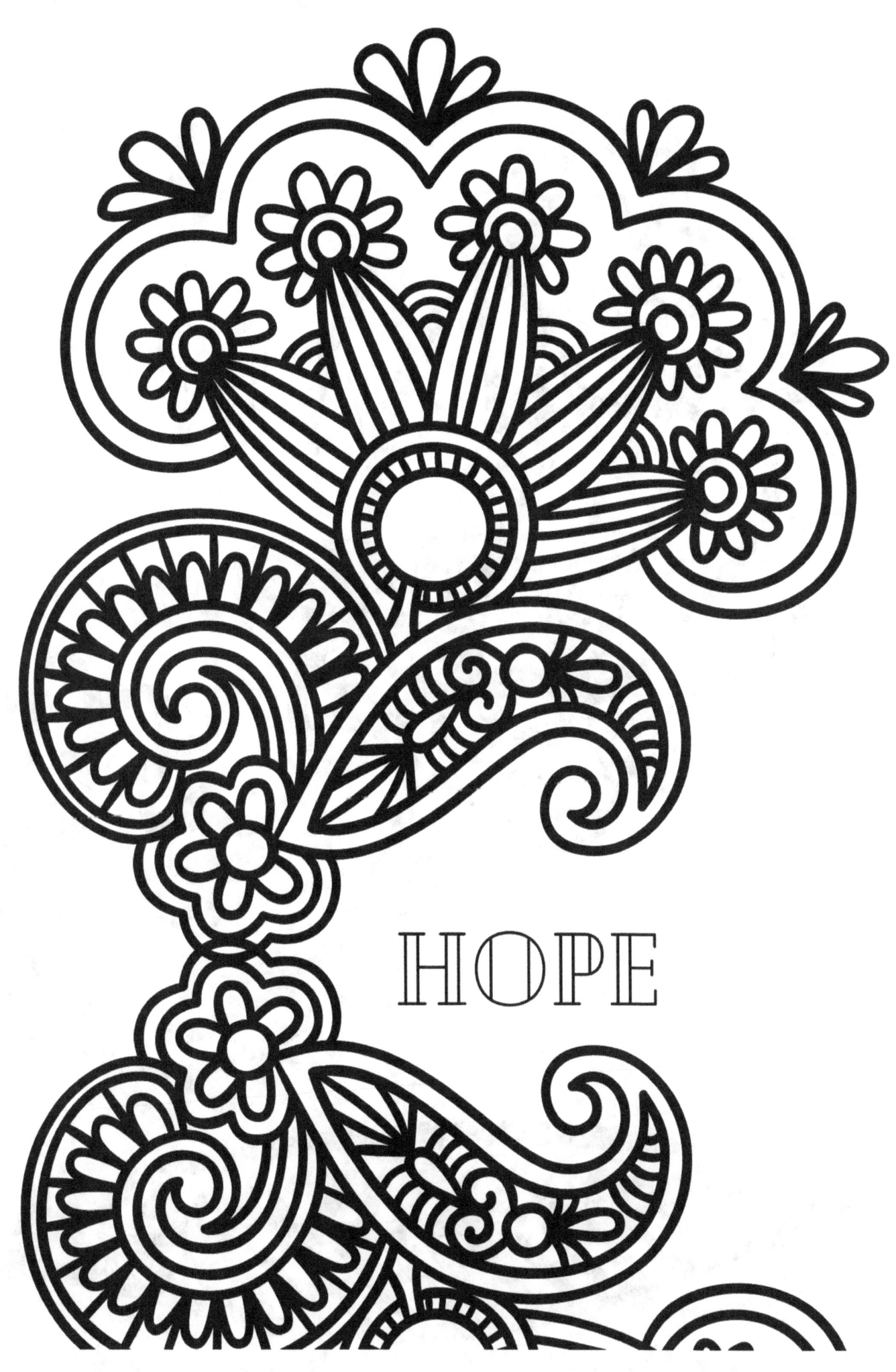

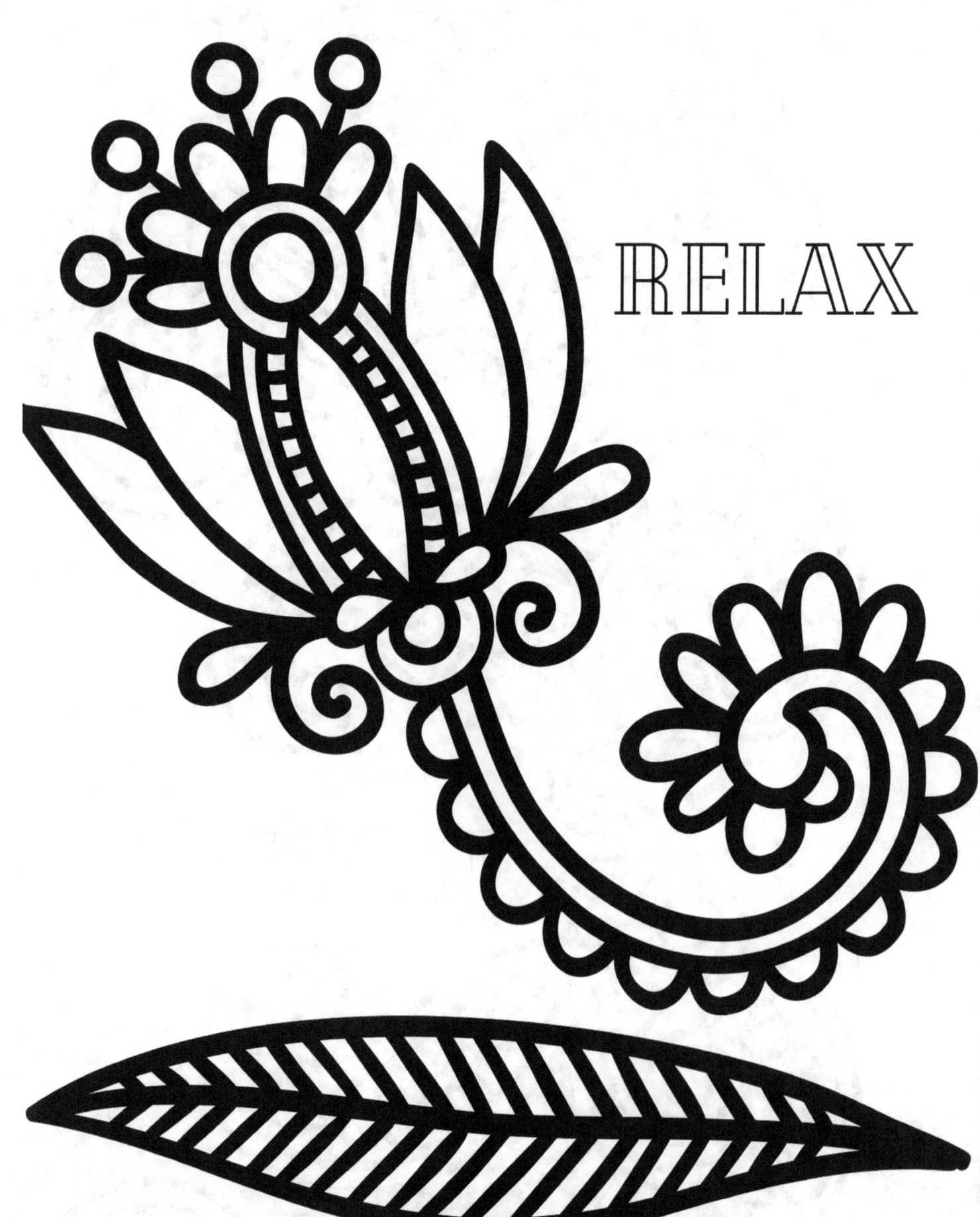

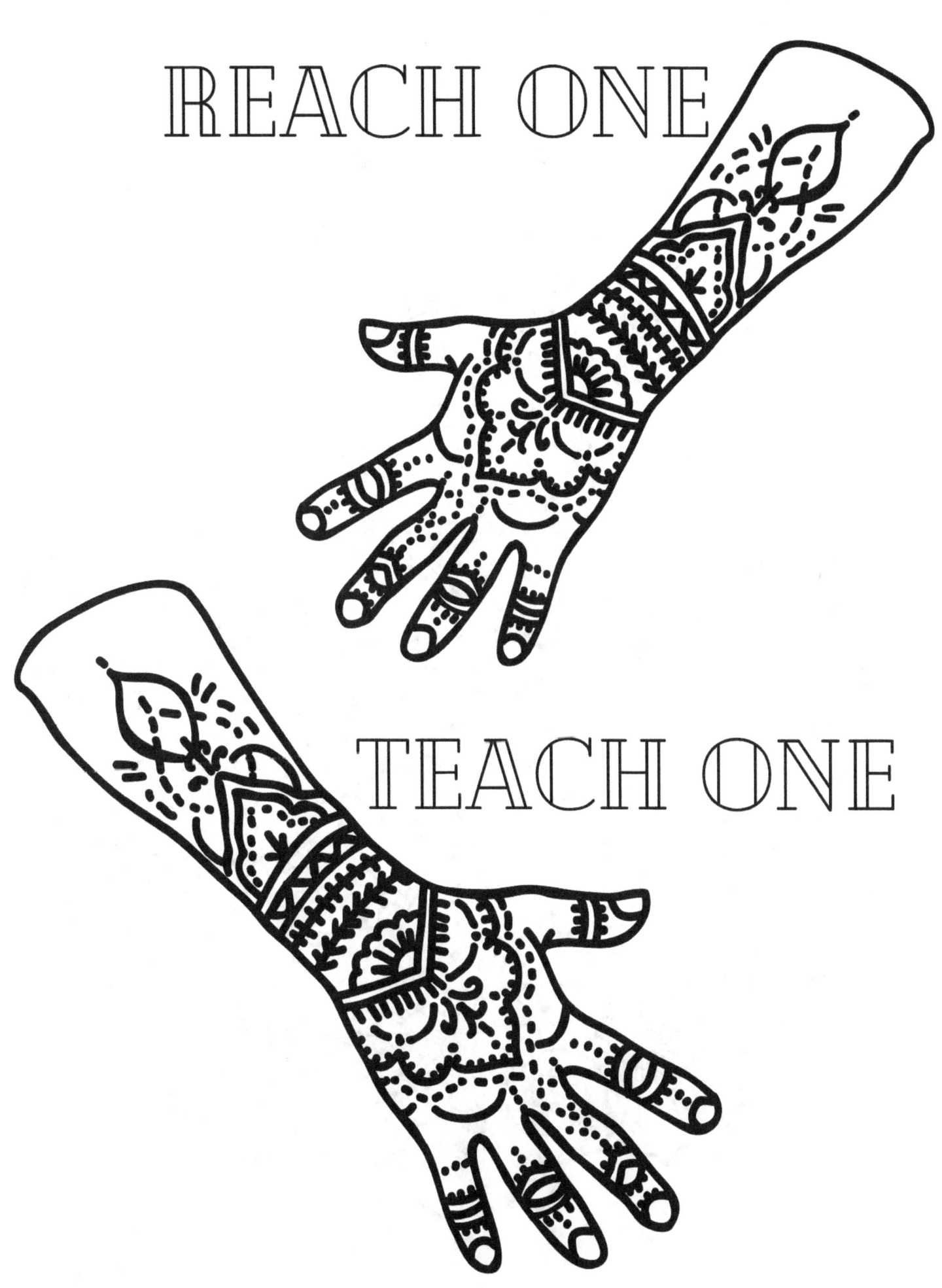

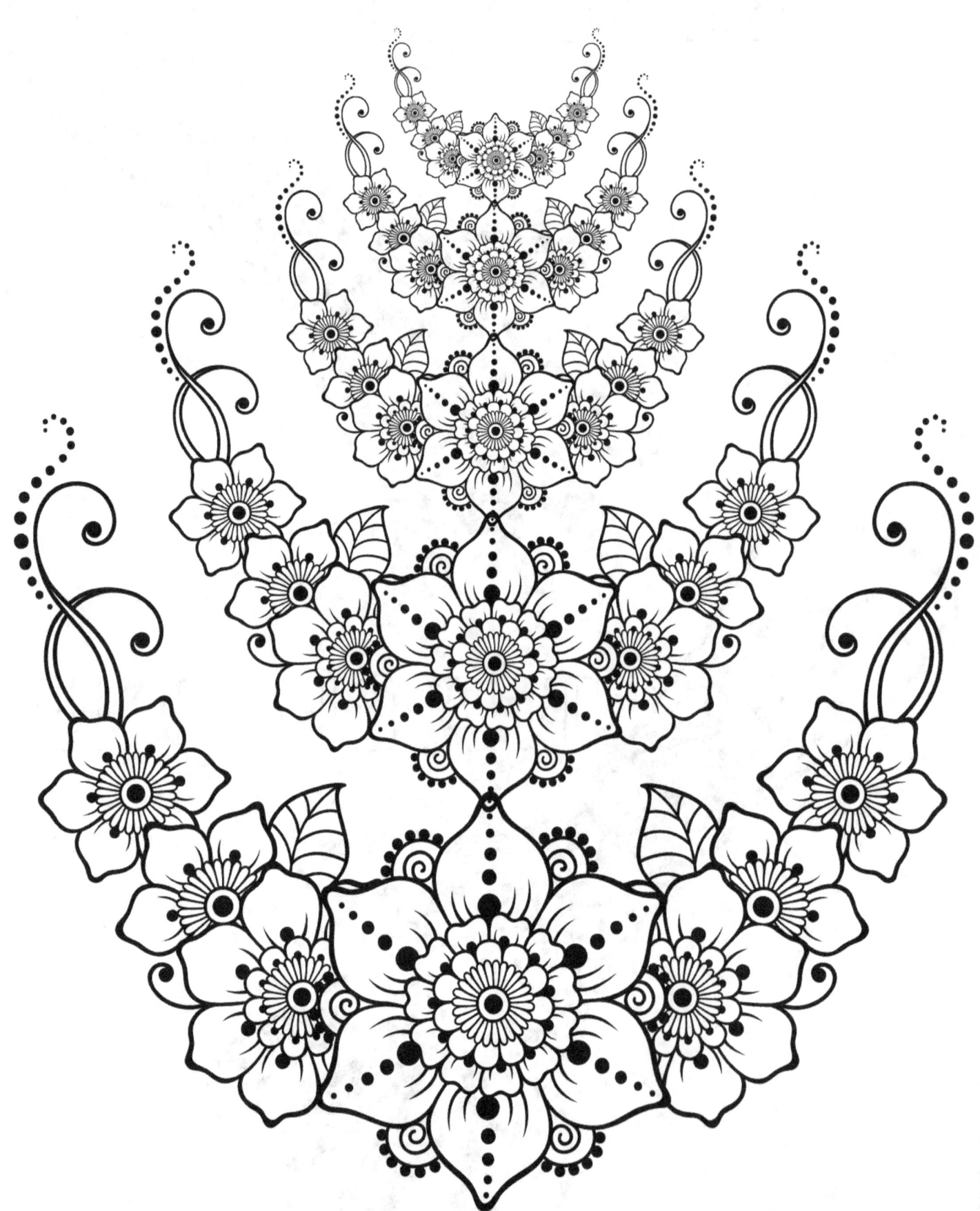

STAND TALL

REFLECT

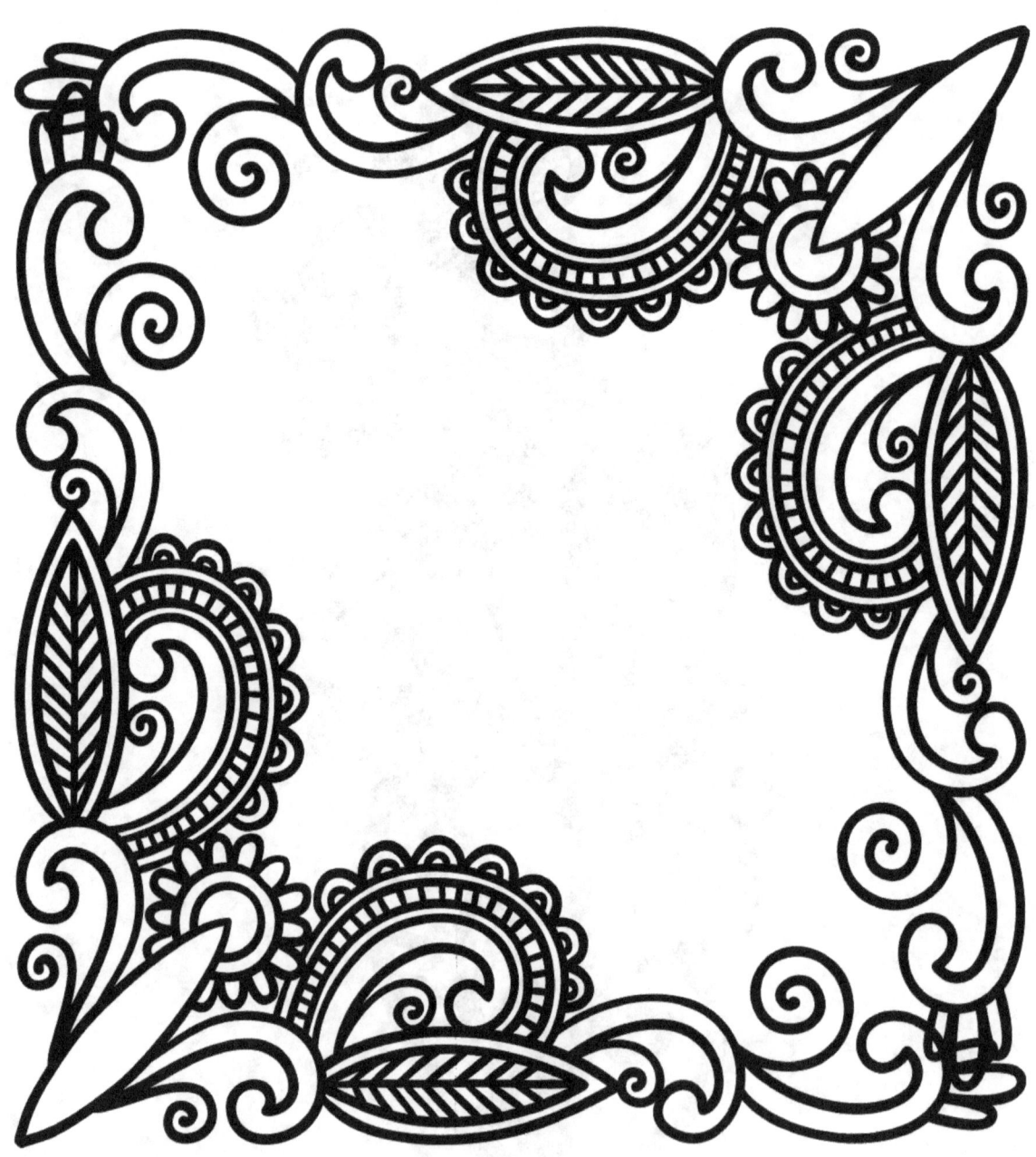

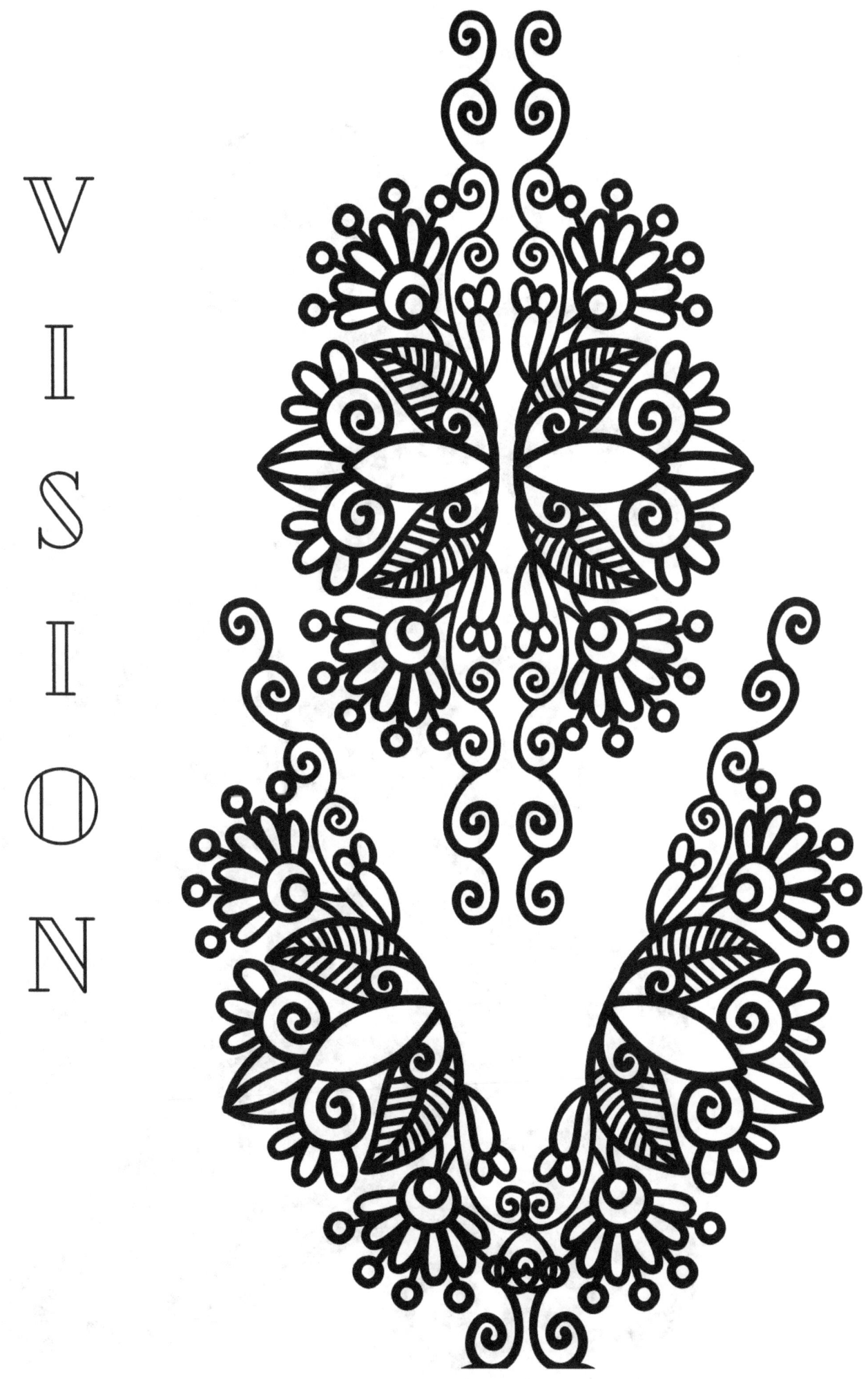

VISION

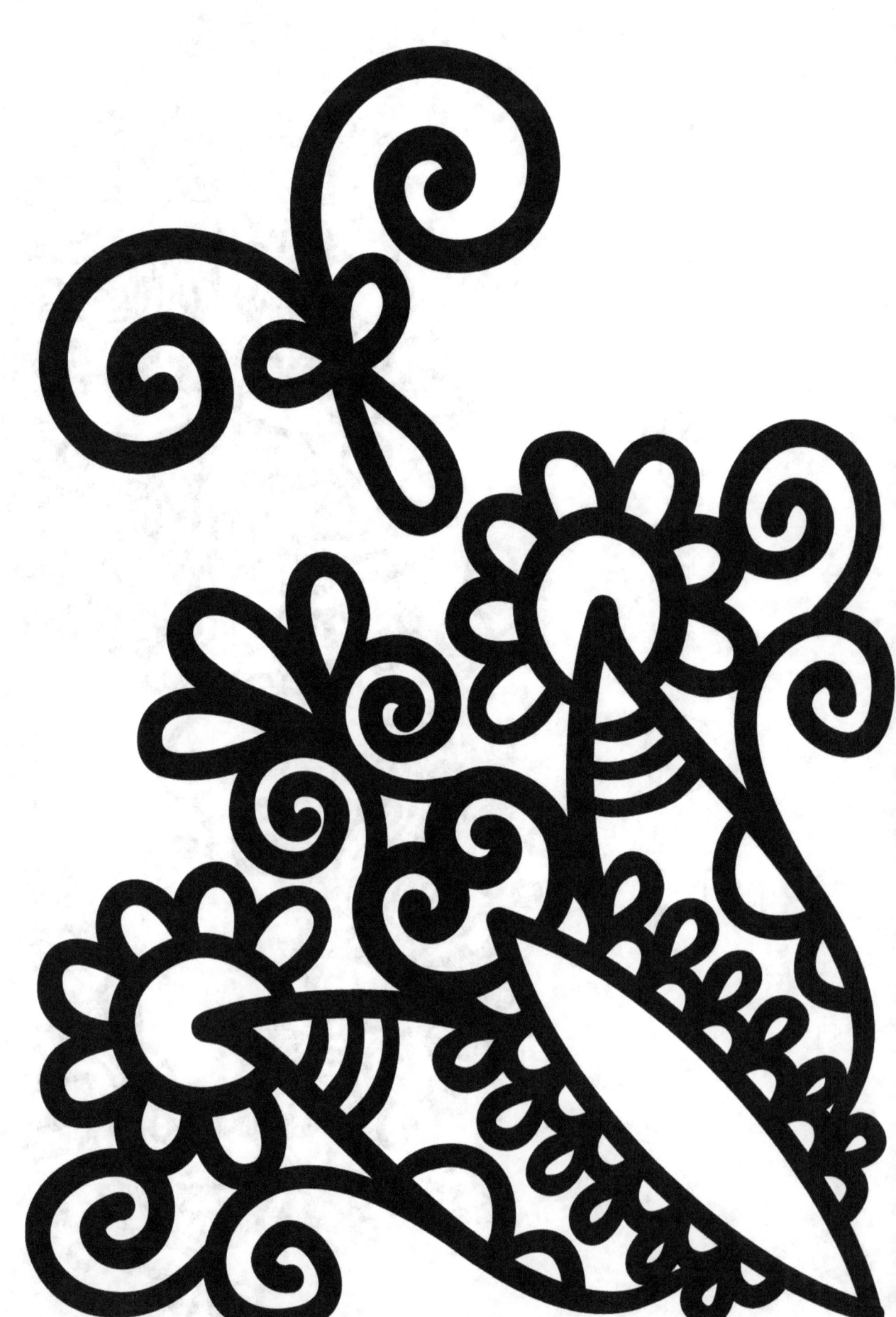

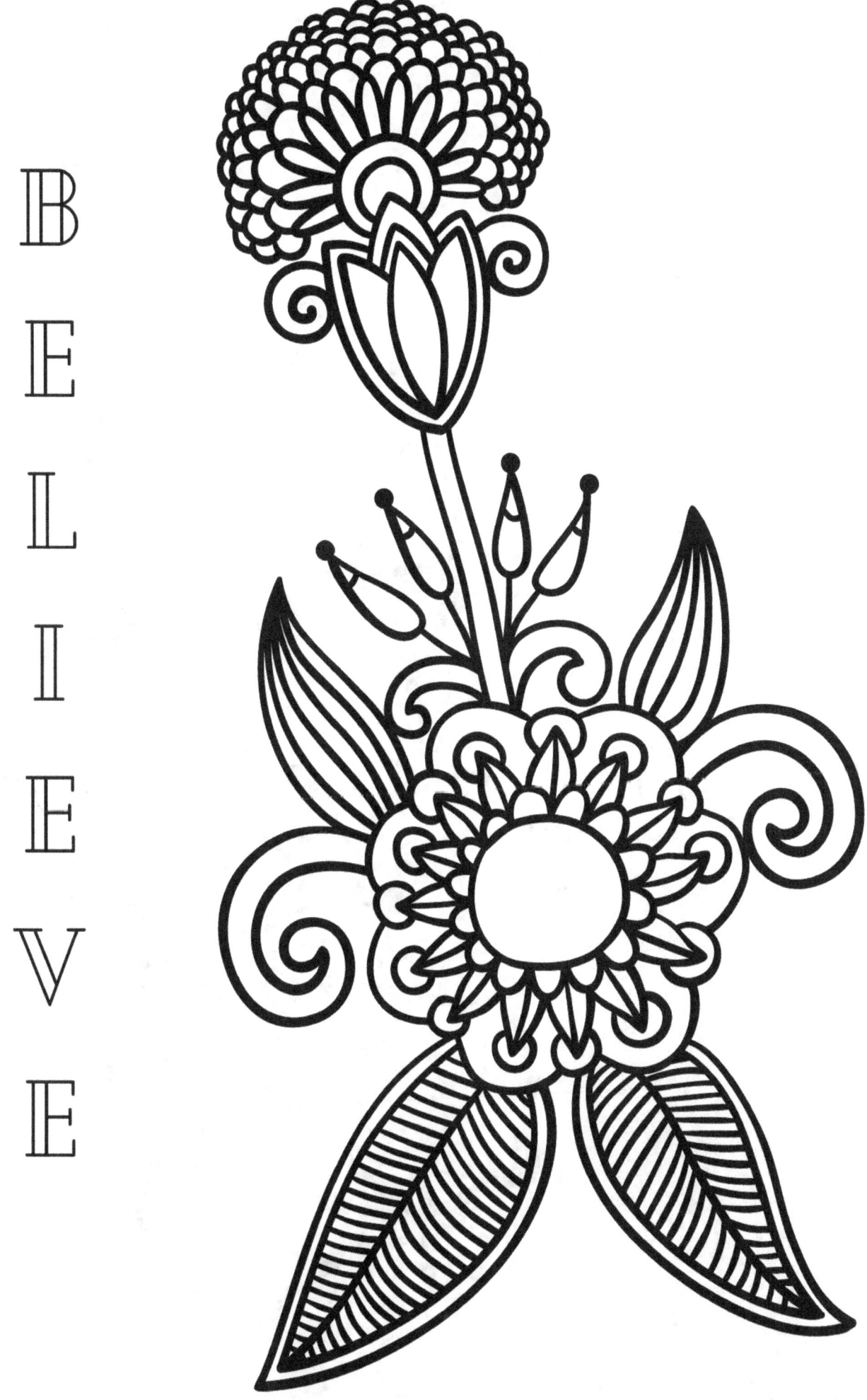

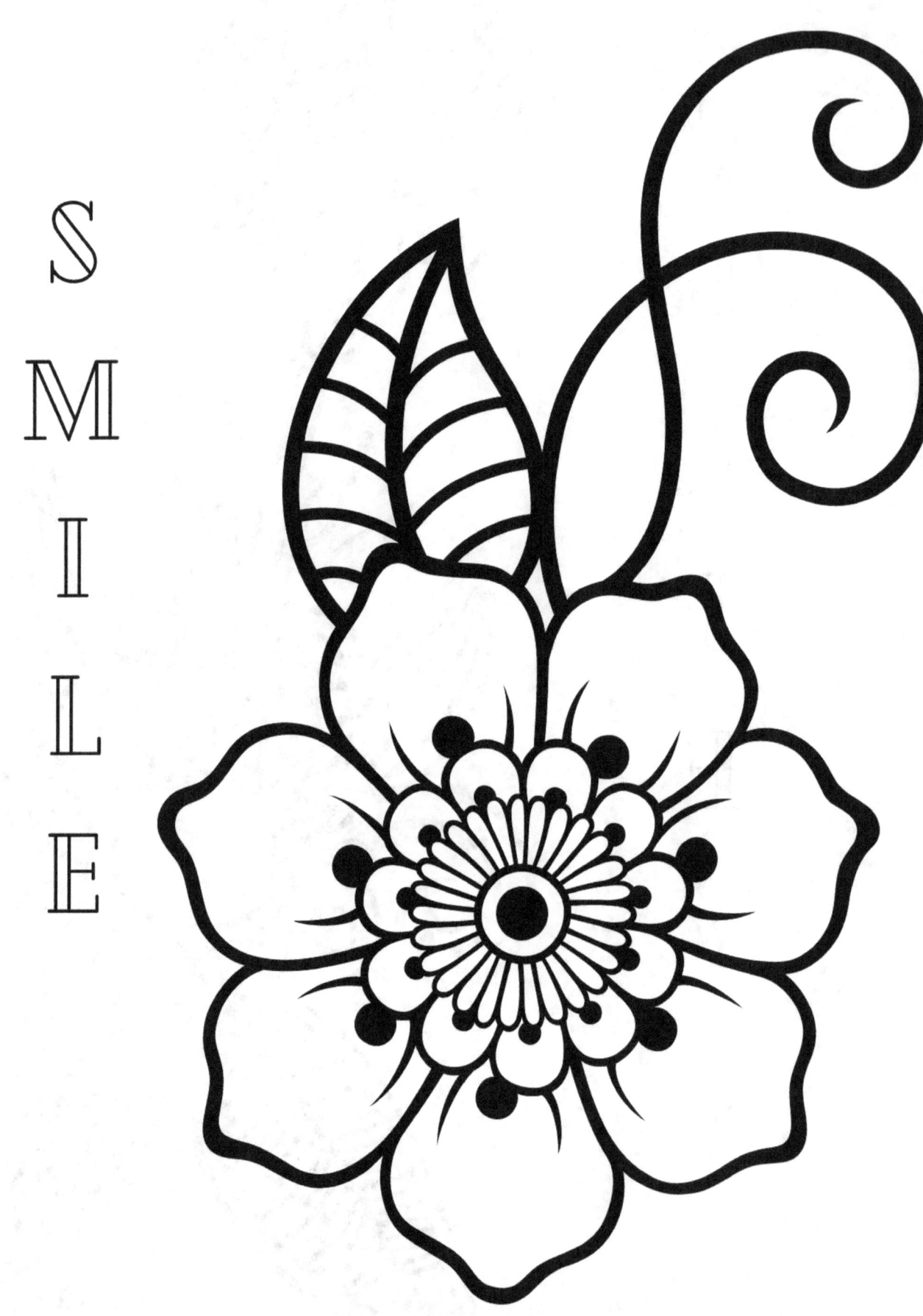

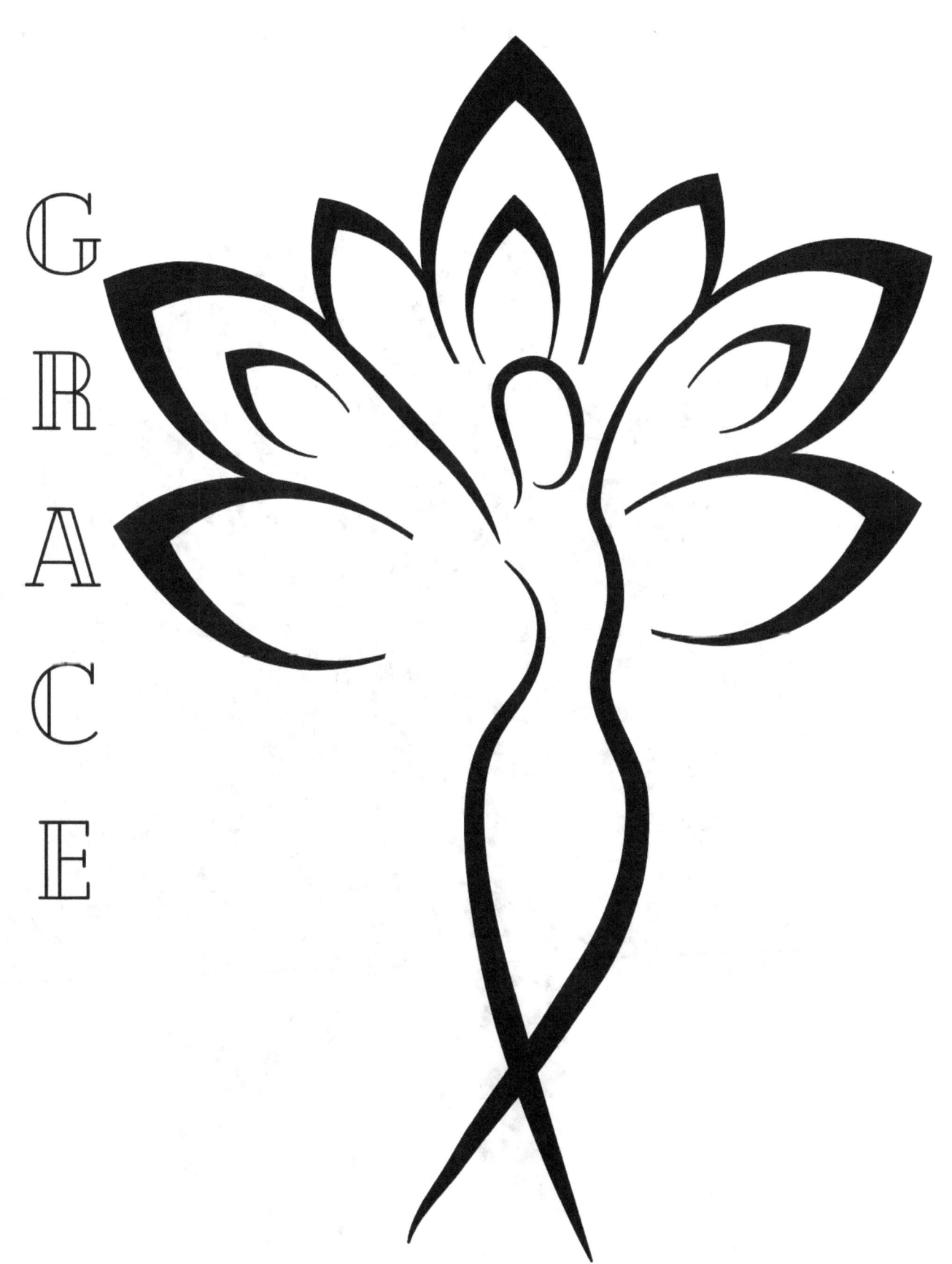

GROWTH

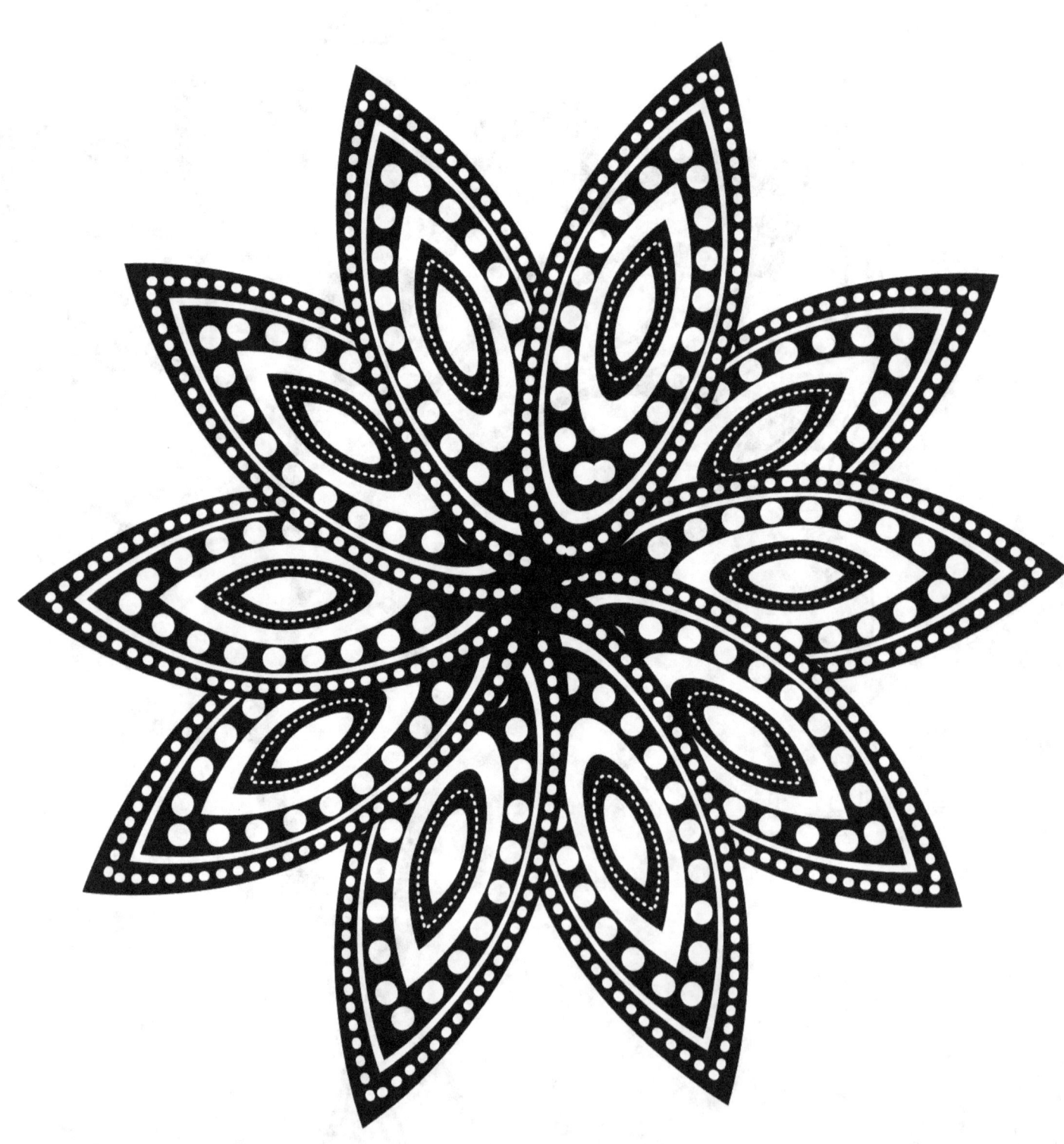

I AM BEAUTIFUL

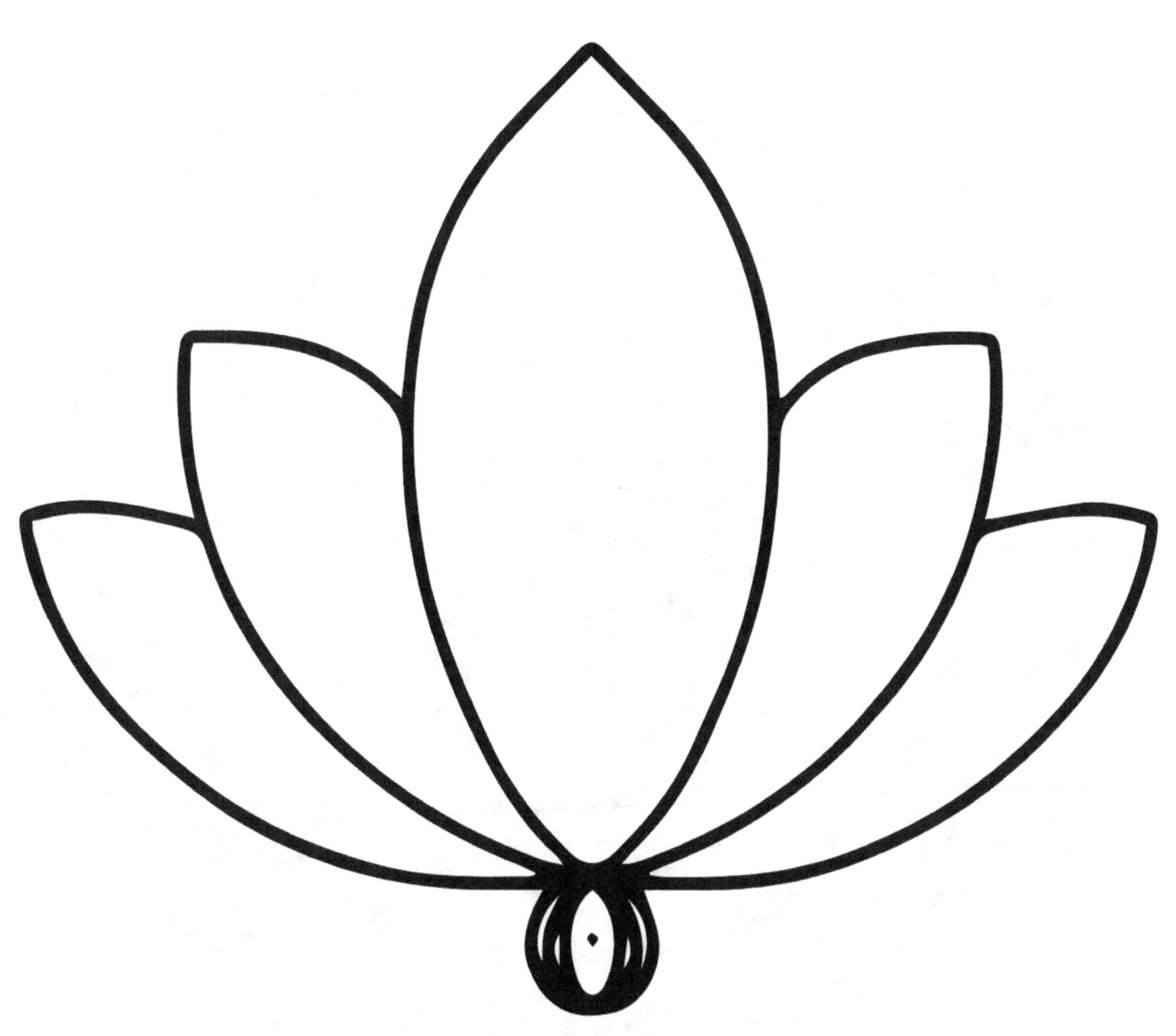

I AM HEARD

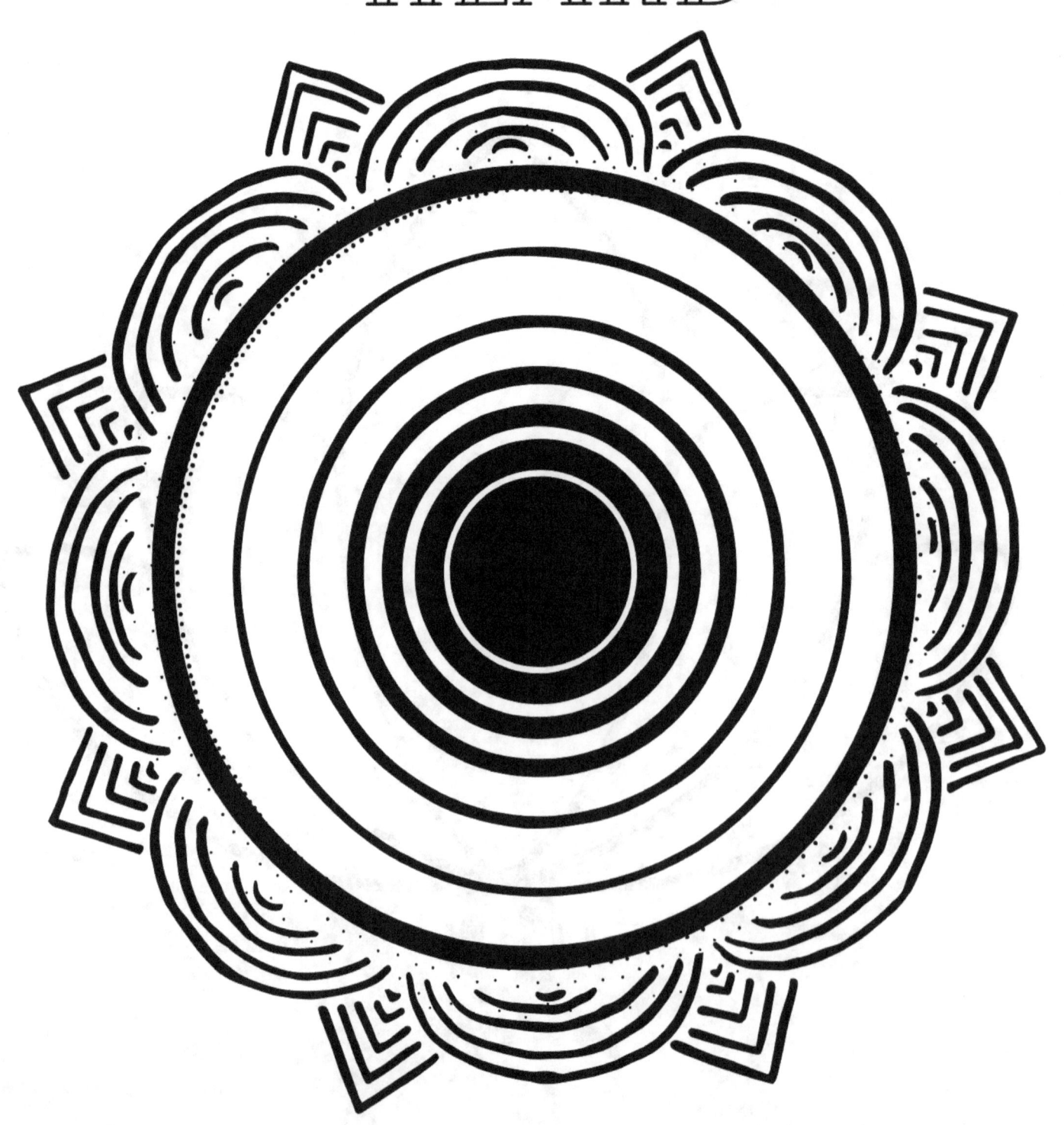

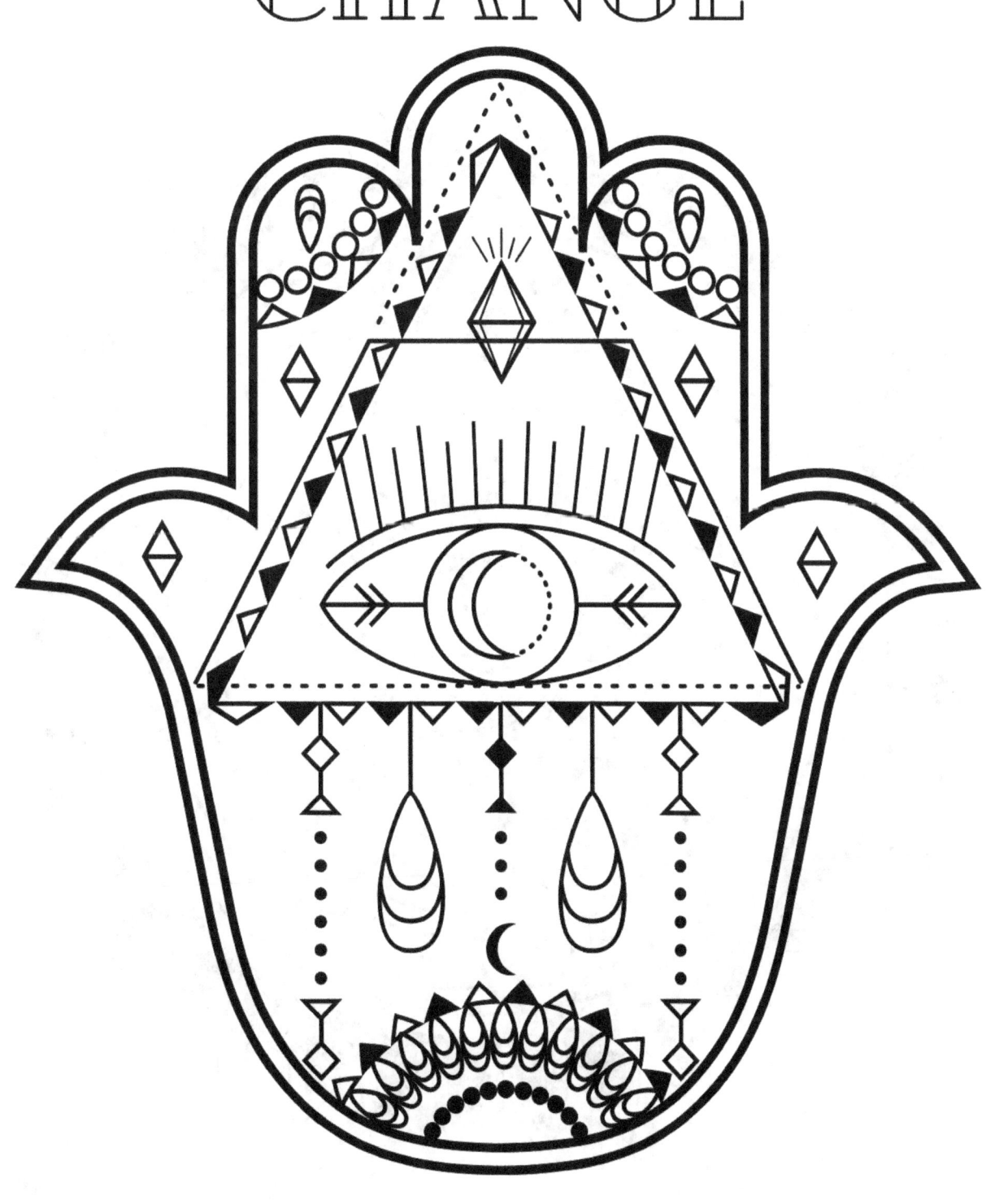

I WELCOME GOOD VIBES

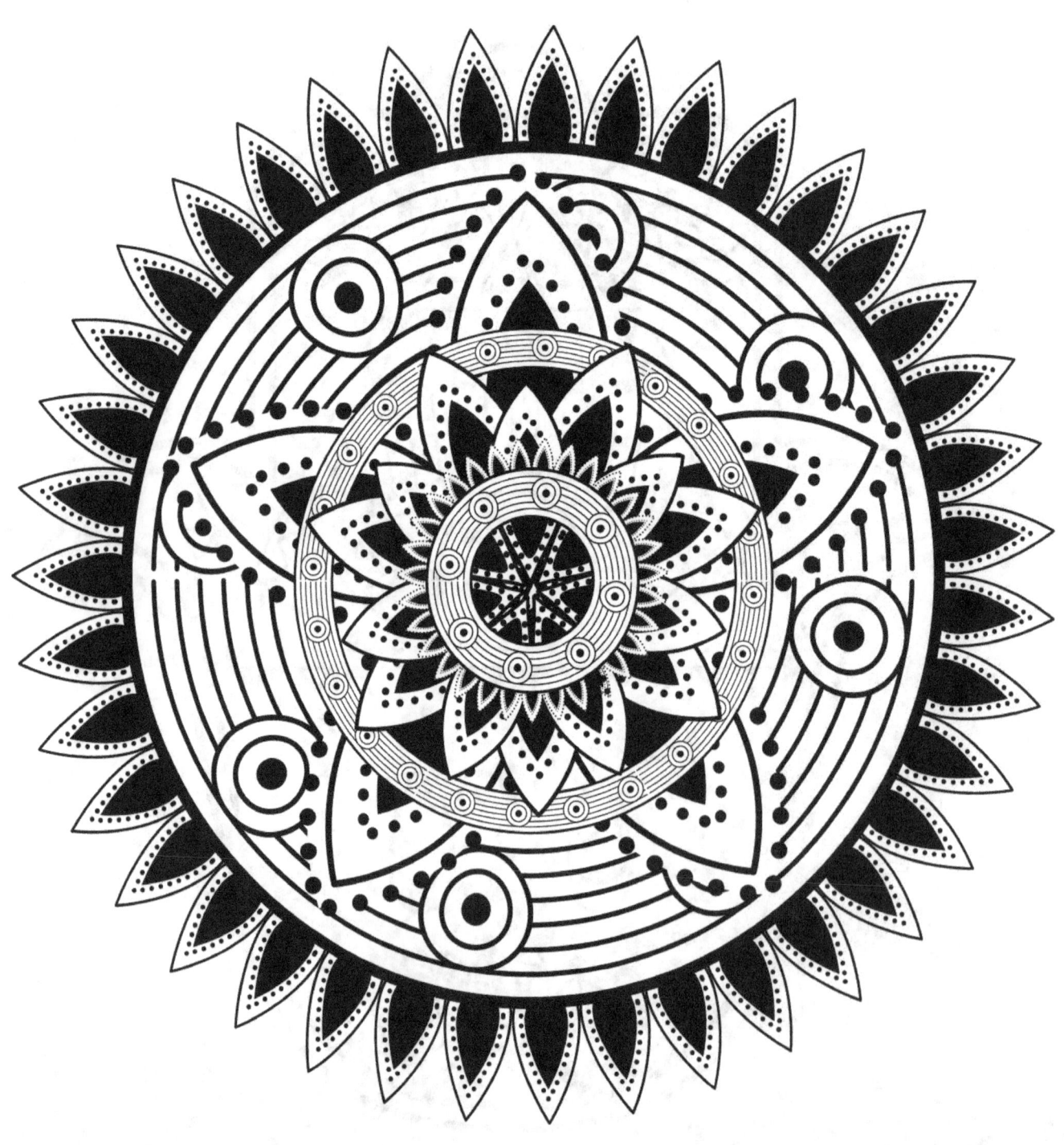

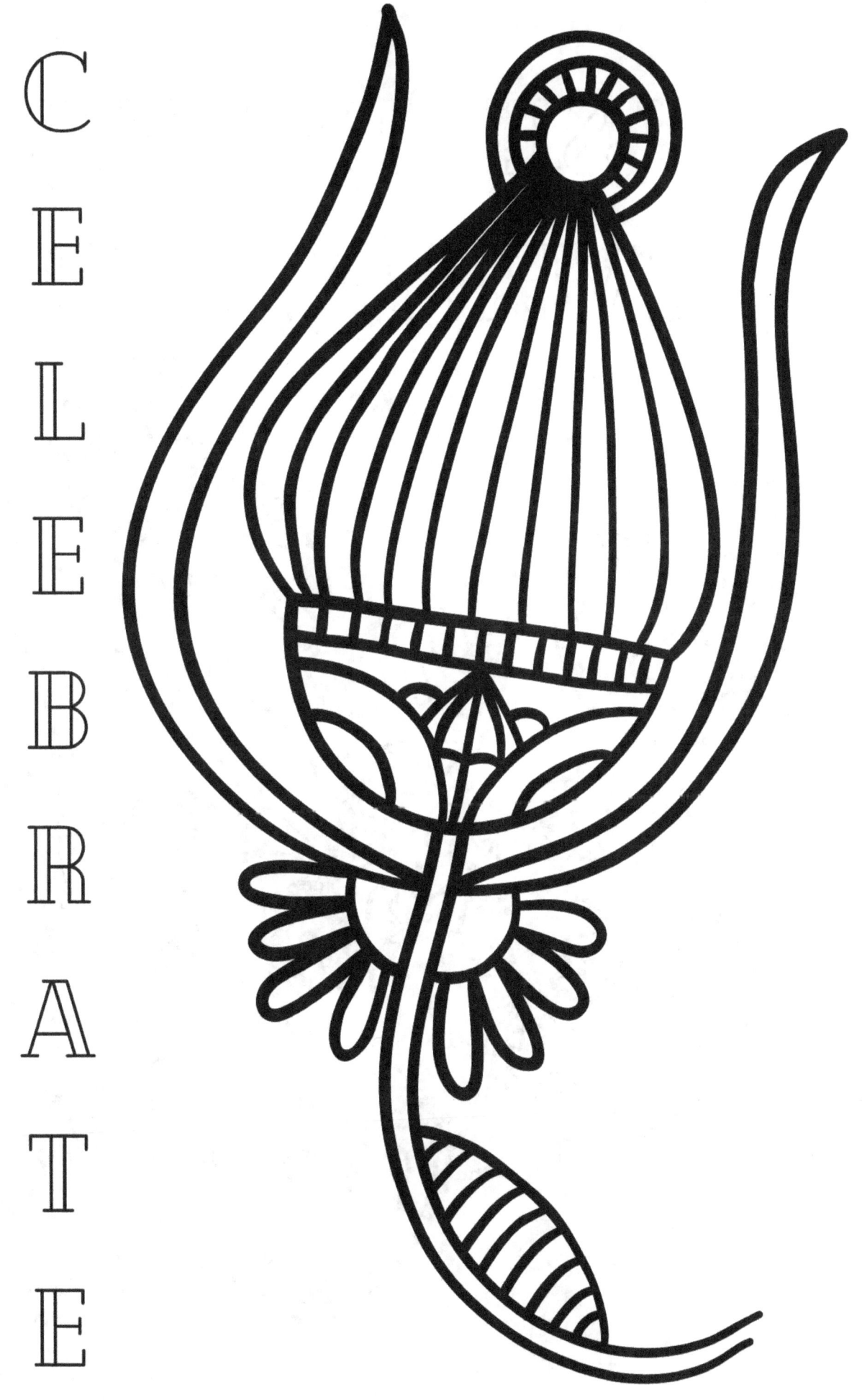

I SEE BEAUTY EVERYWHERE

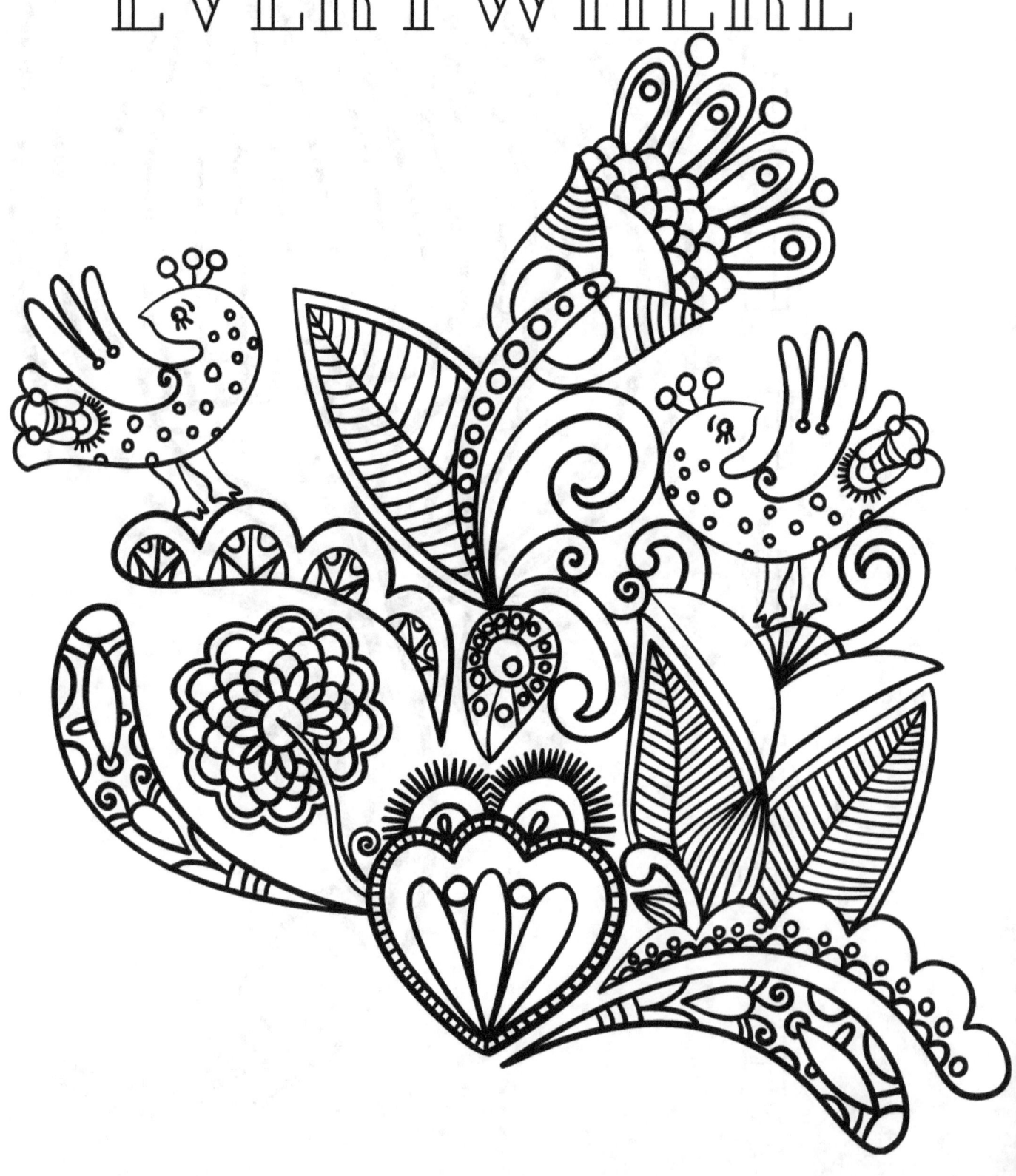

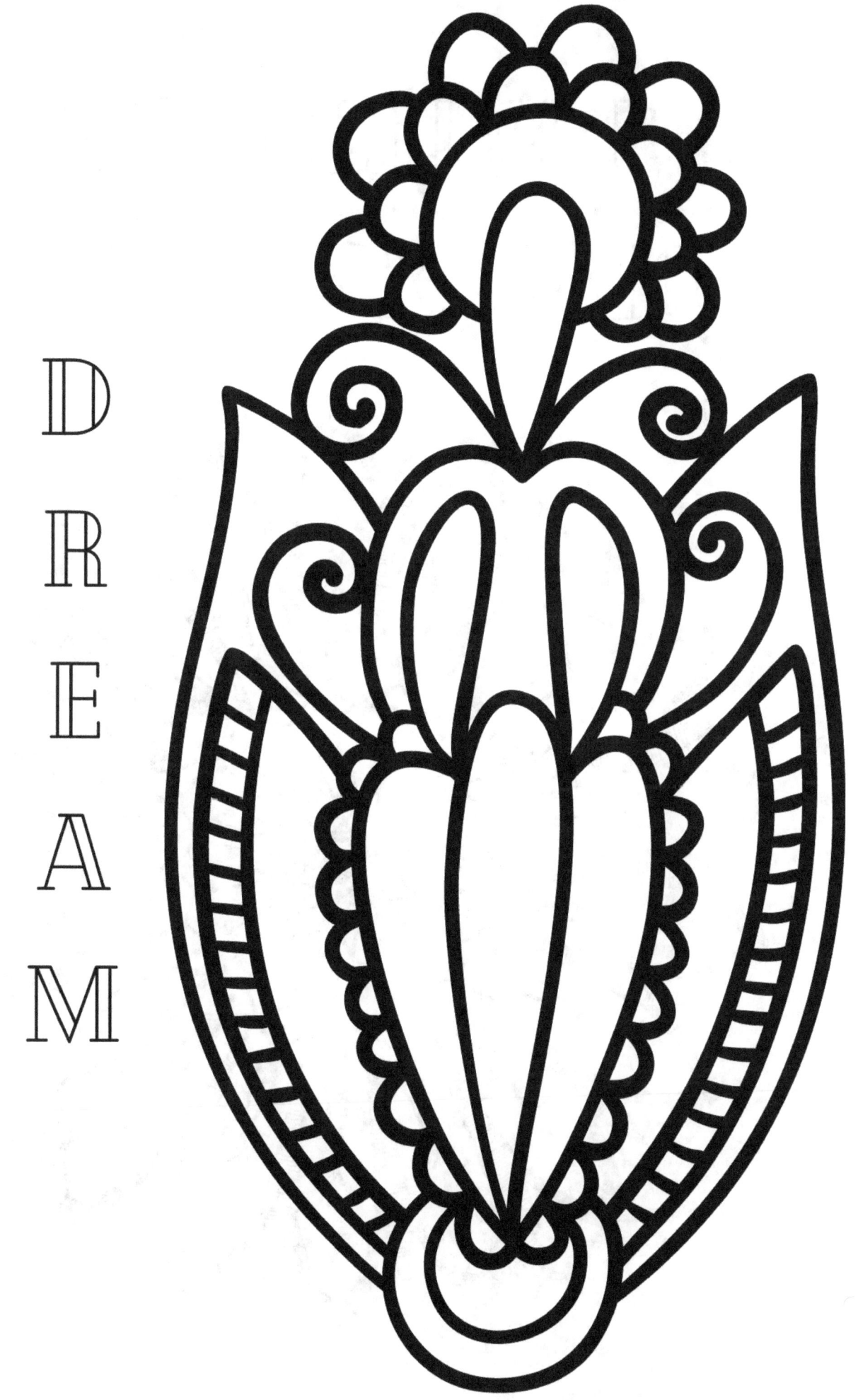

I WILL NOT DIM MY LIGHT

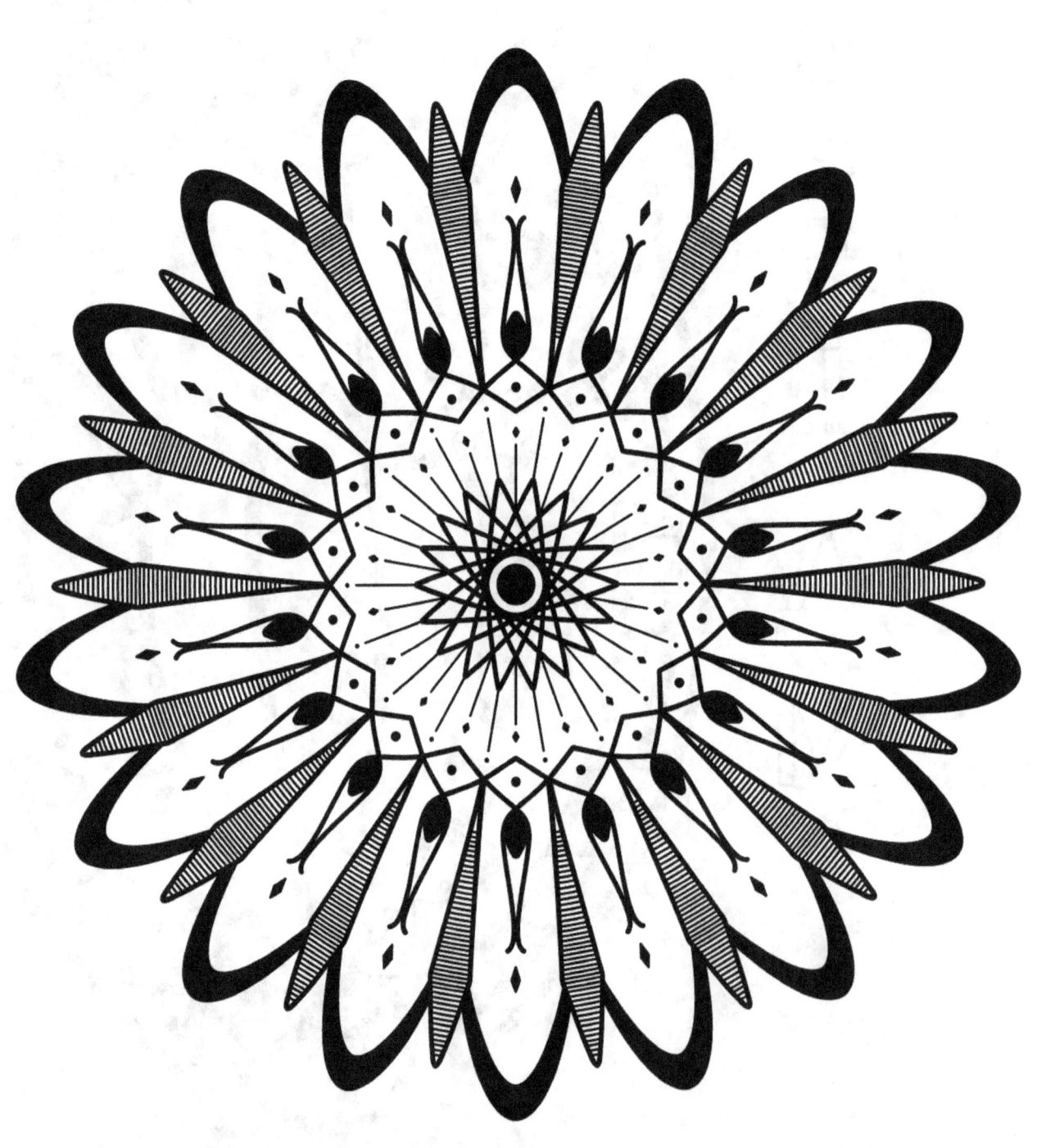

MY FUTURE IS PROMISING

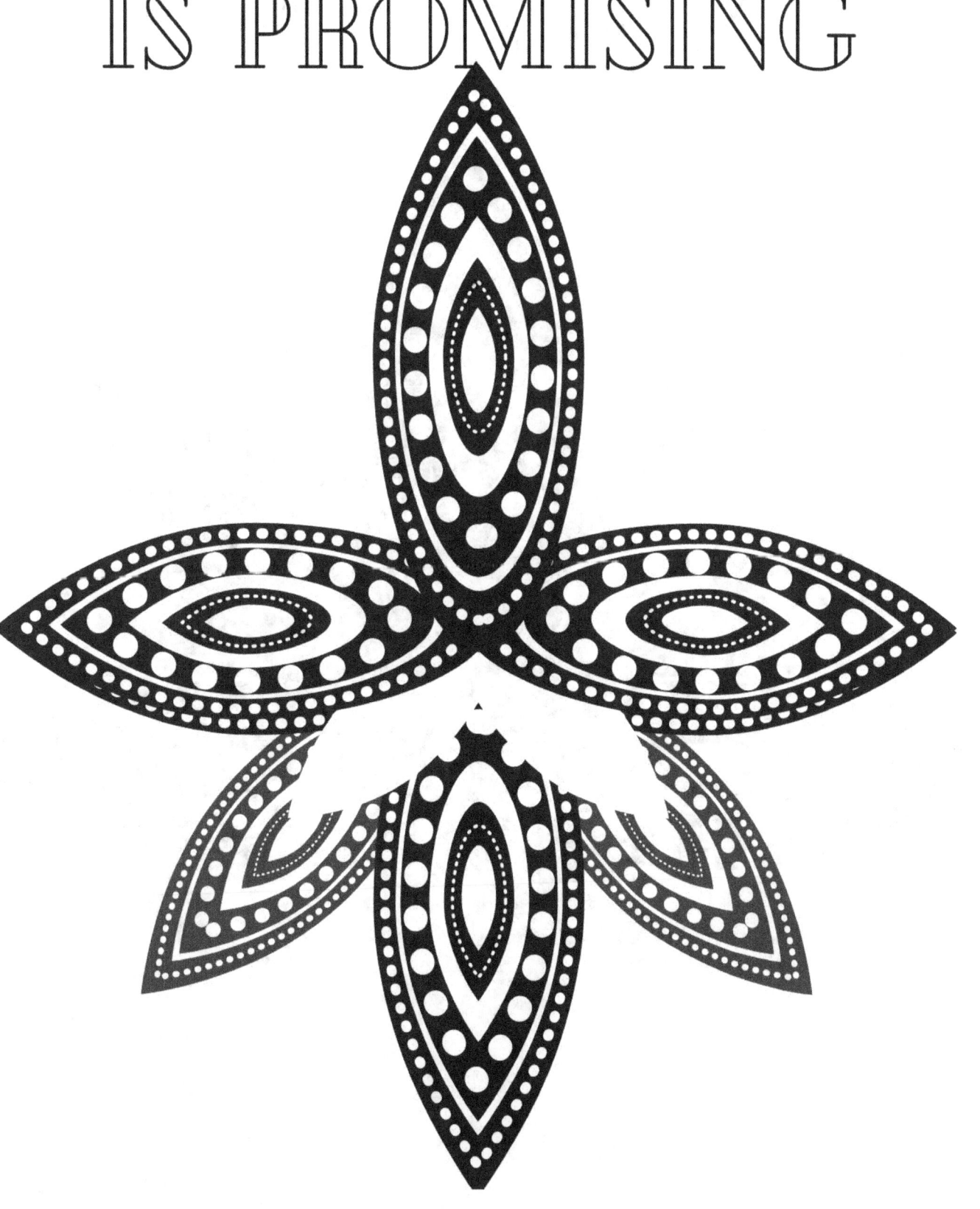

I ALLOW PEACE IN MY SPACE

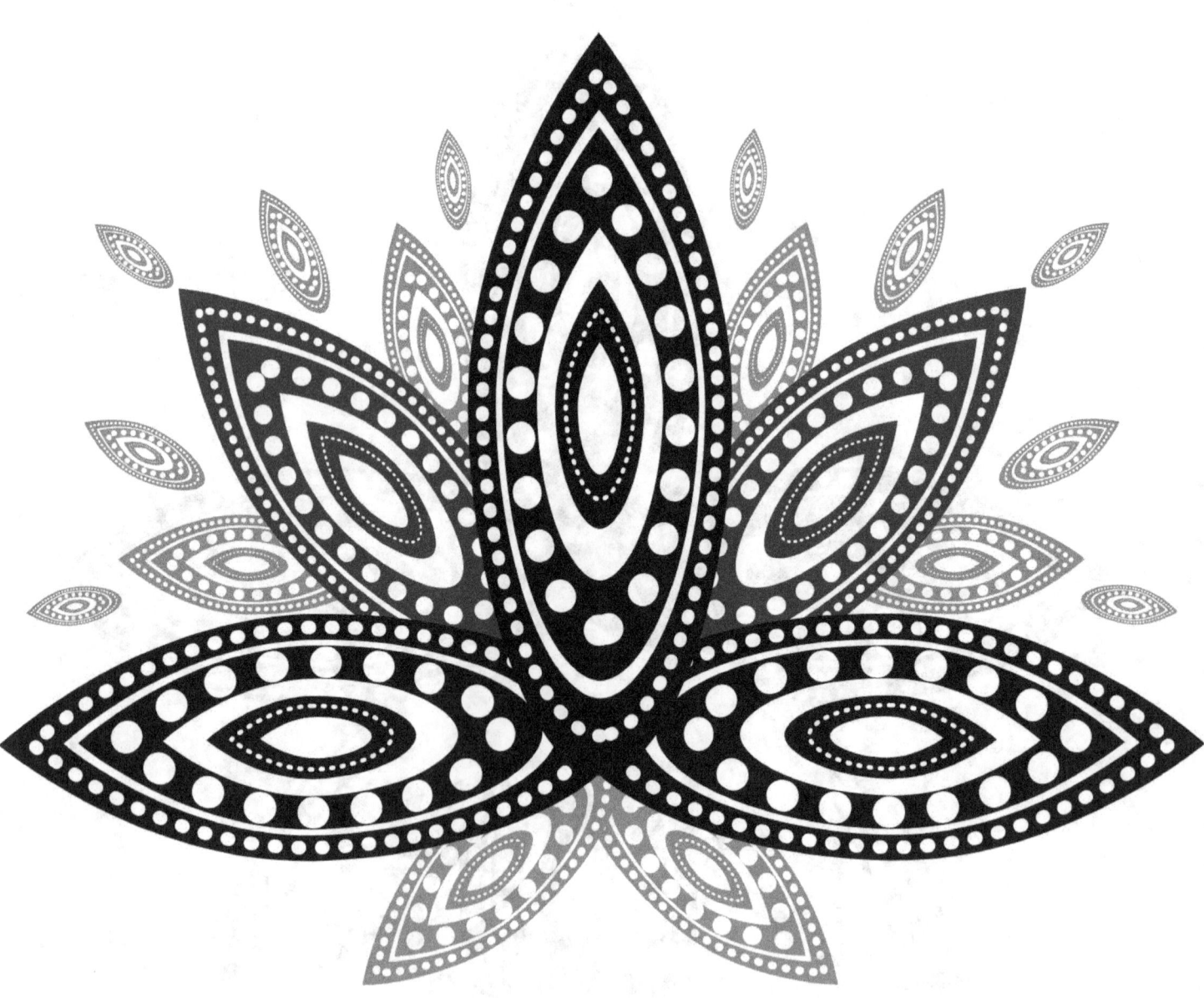

I AM RELIABLE

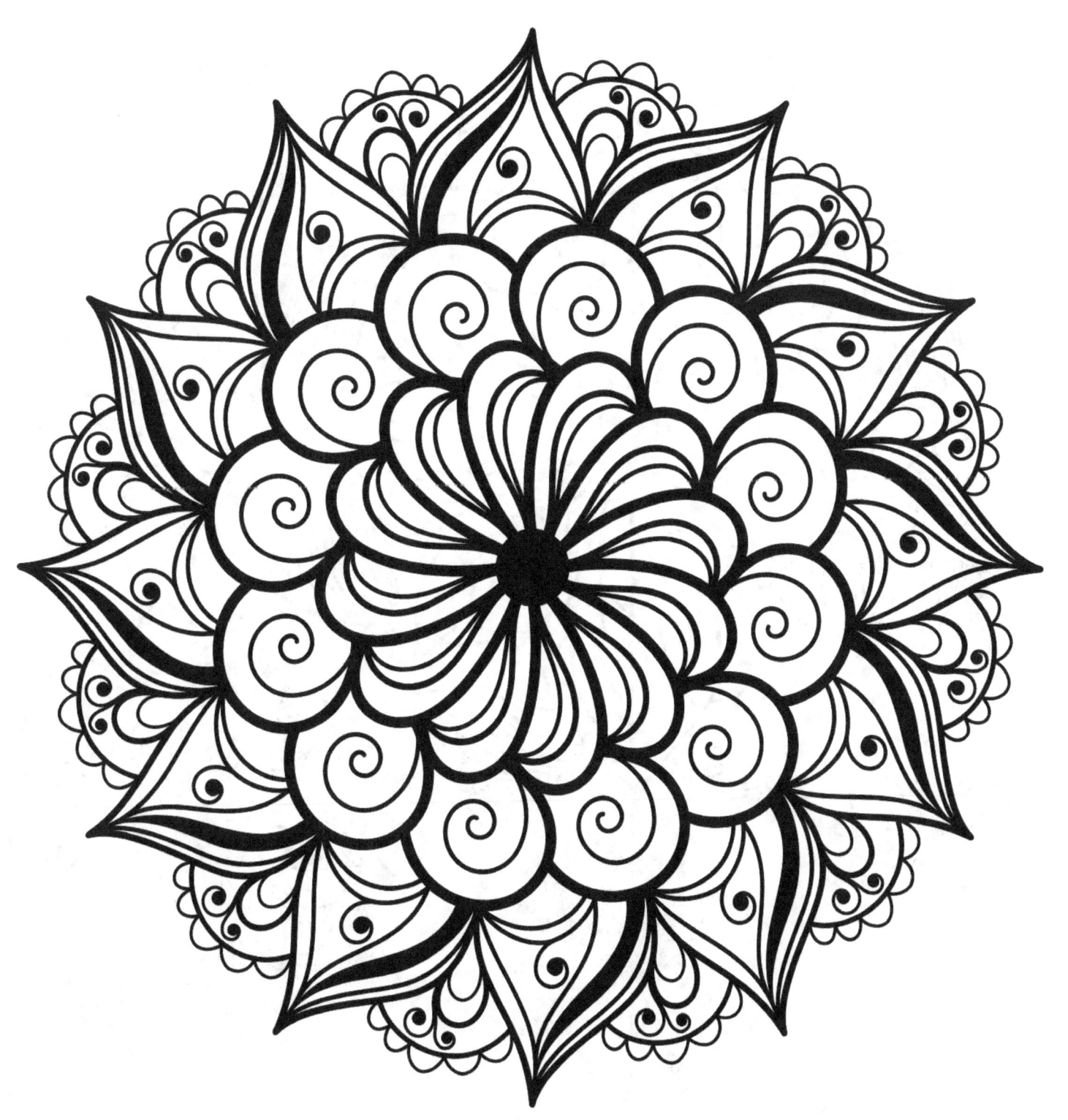

I AM PRESENT

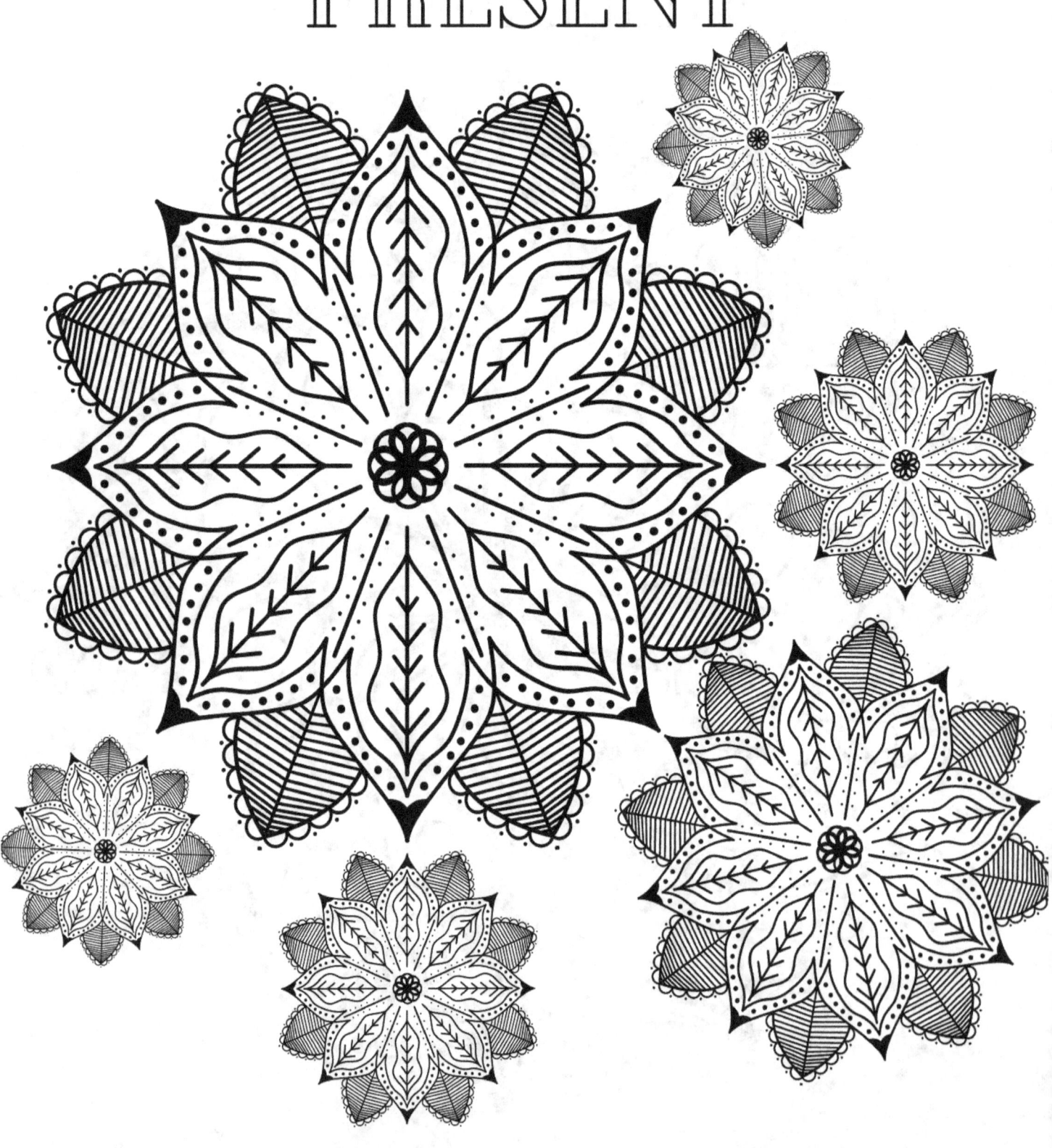

I AM SELF-SUFFICIENT

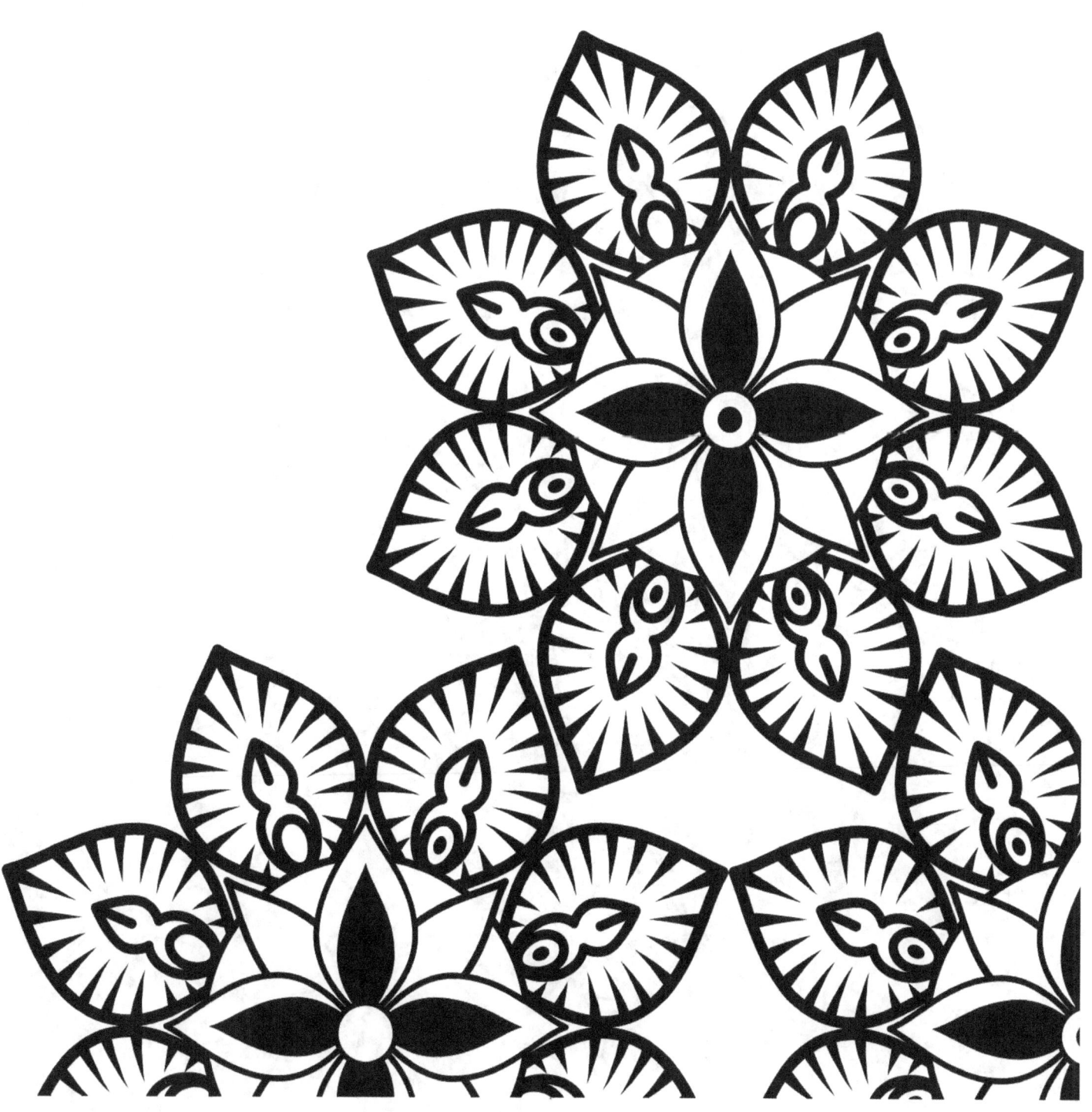

I AM UNIQUE

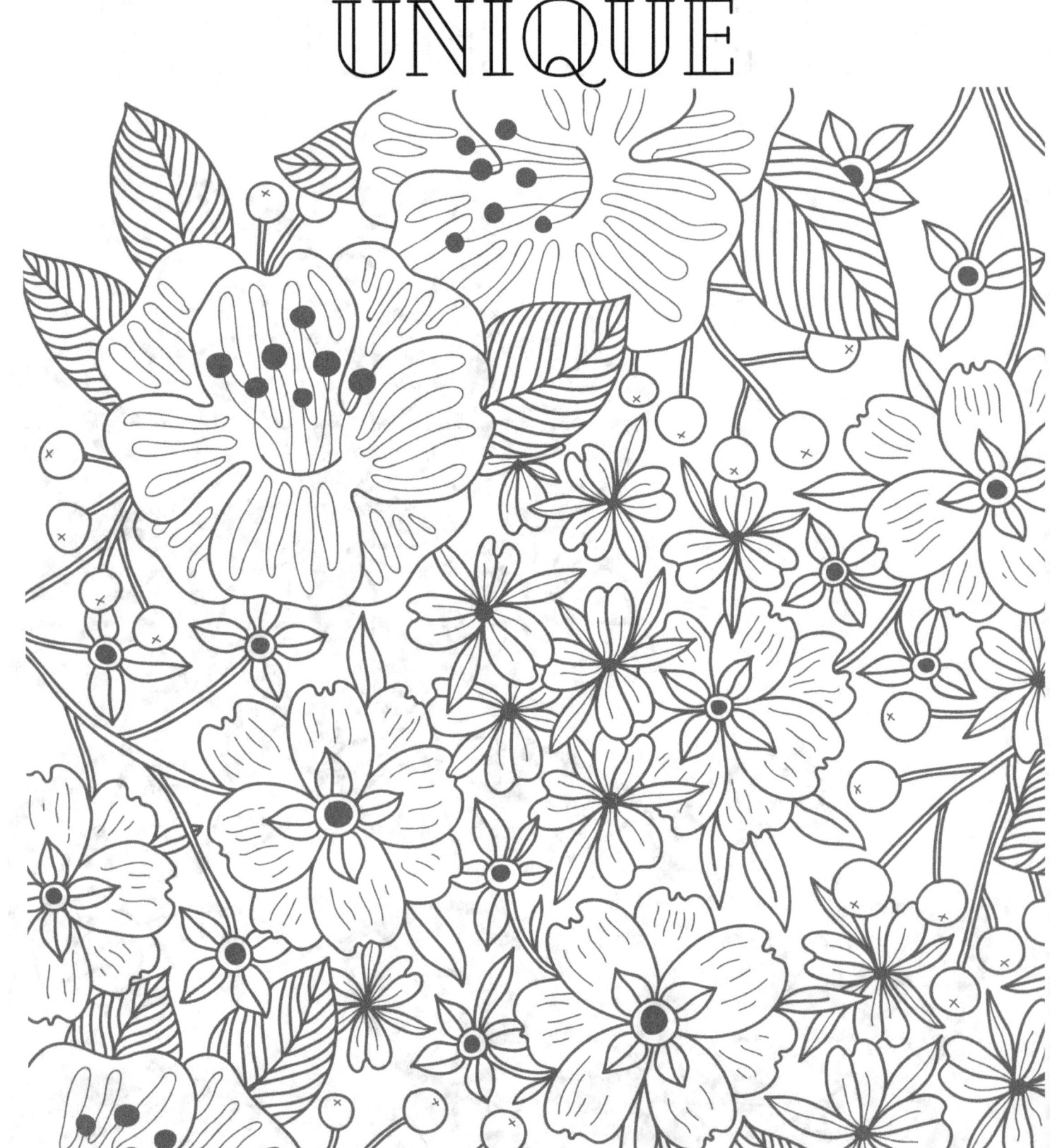

I'M SURROUNDED BY BEAUTY

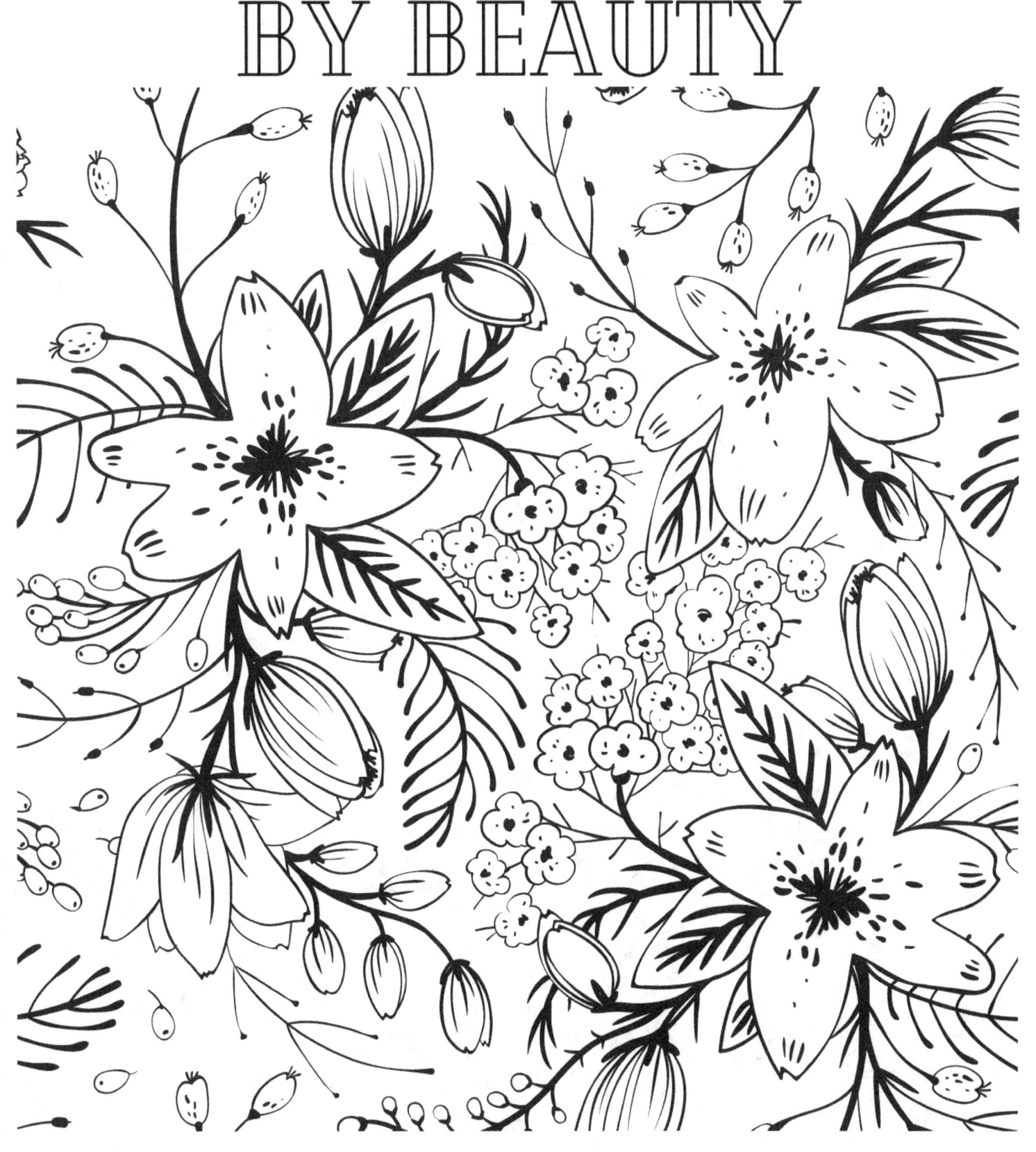

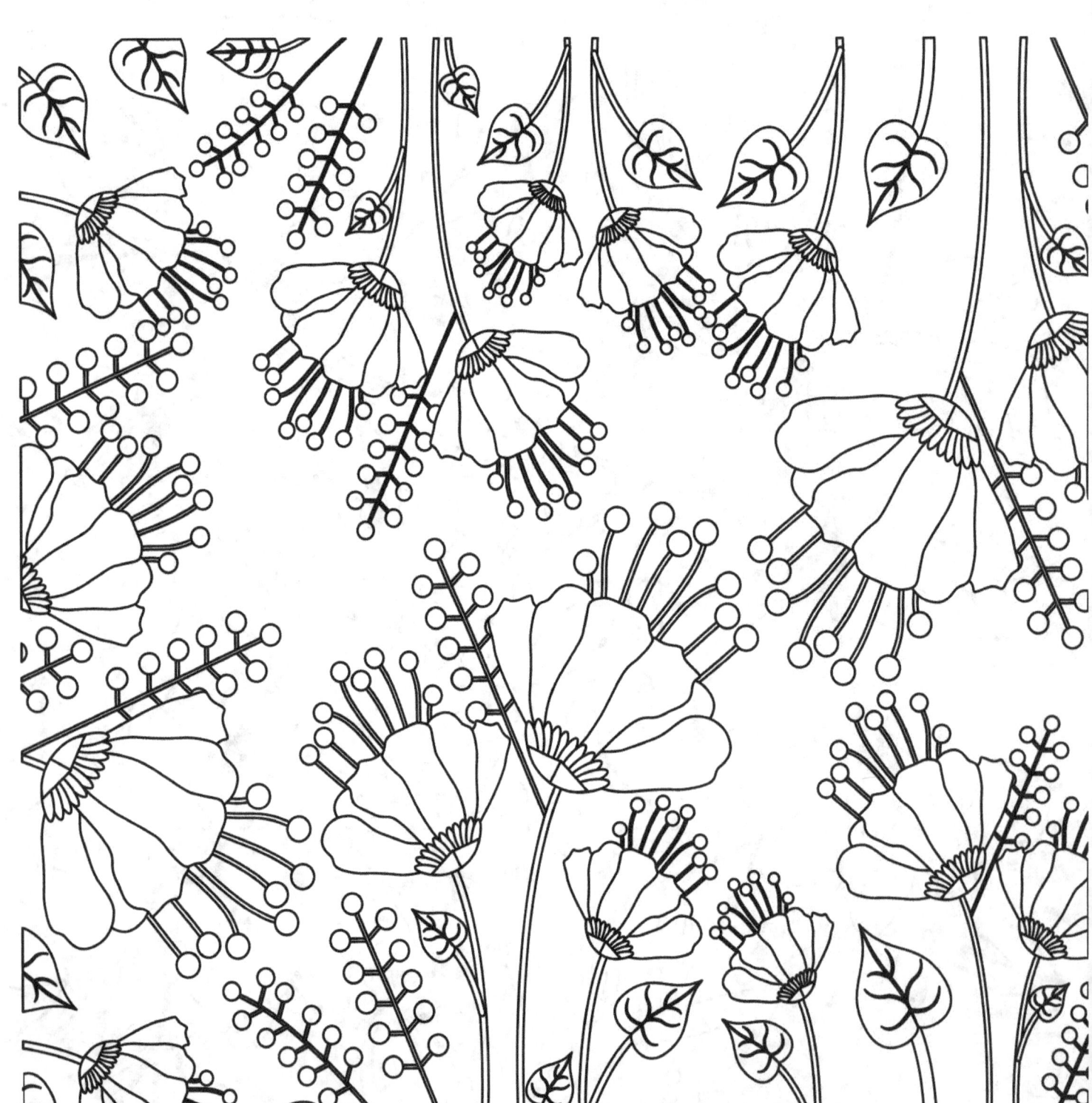

I SEEK

HAPPINESS

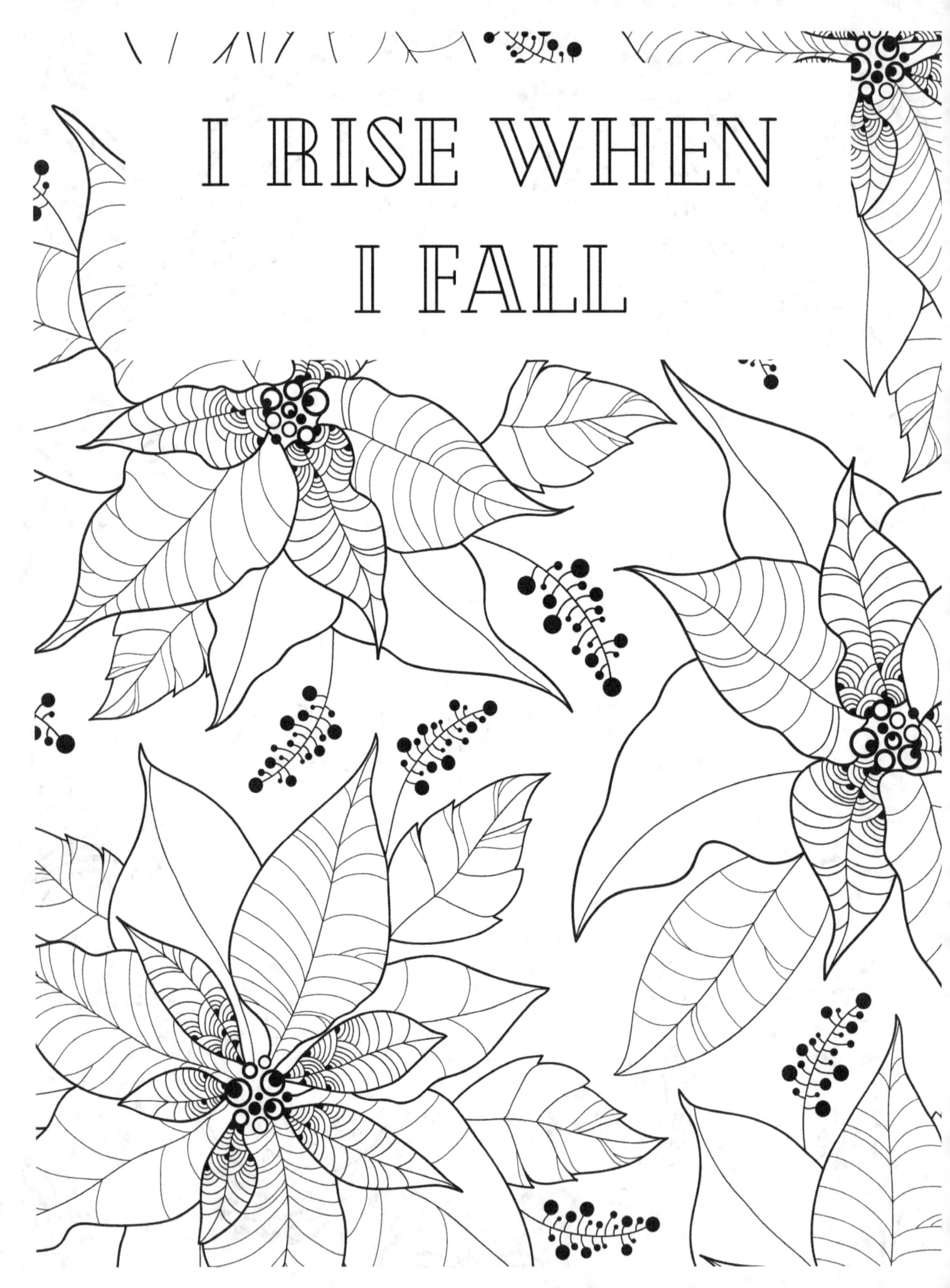

I HAVE SUPPORT

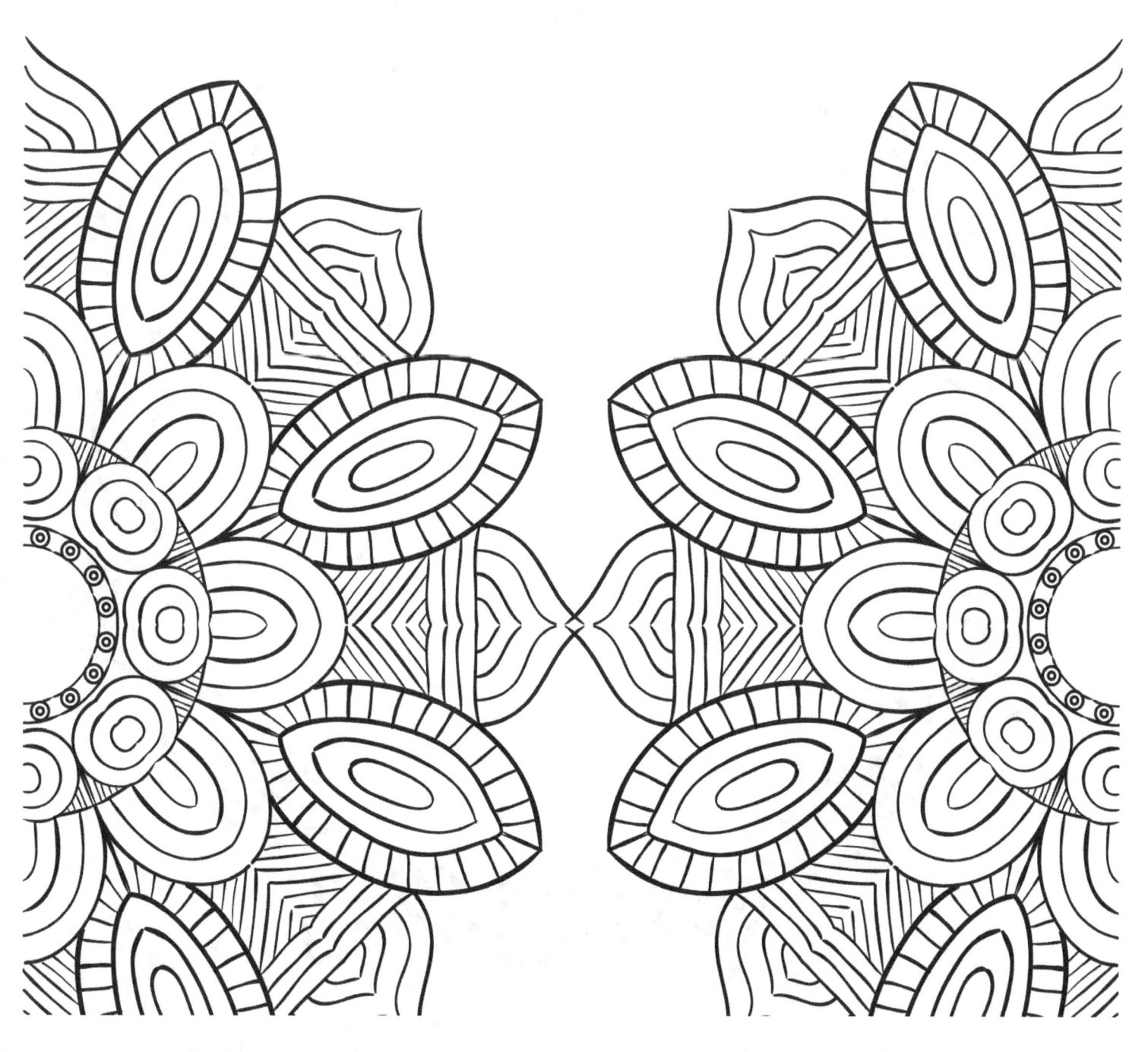

I AM CENTERED

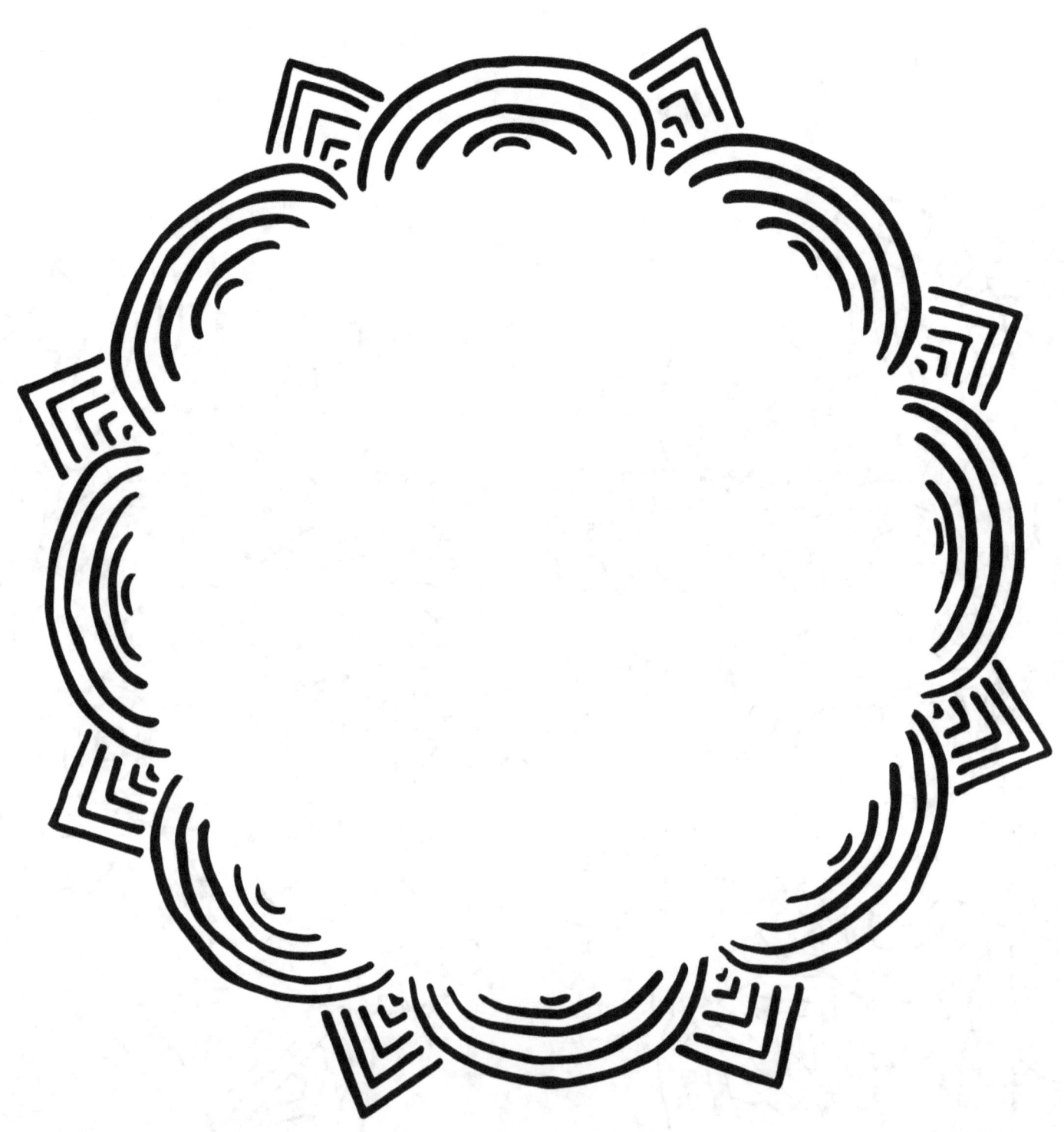

I AM HUMBLED

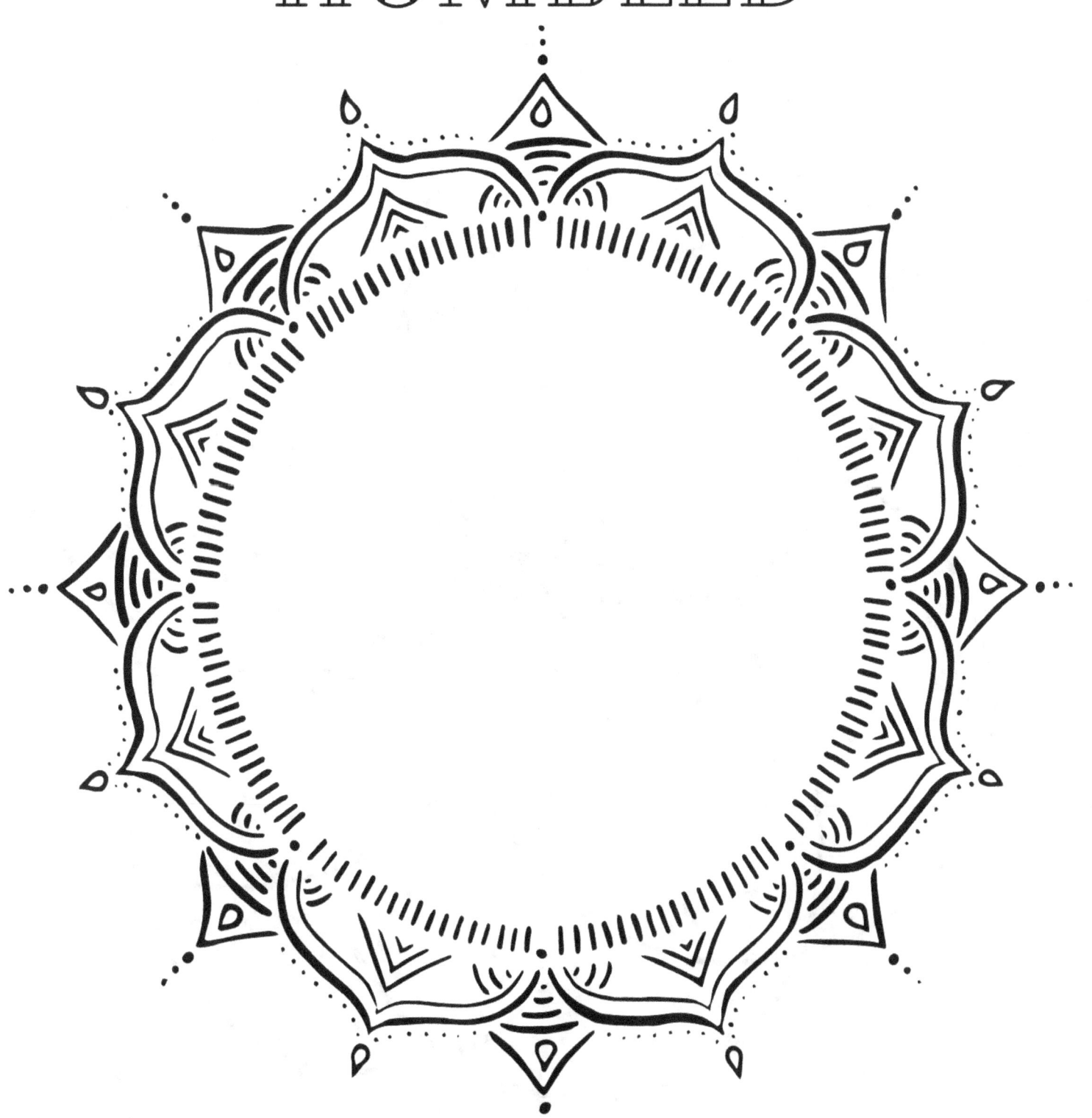

I AM EVERYTHING

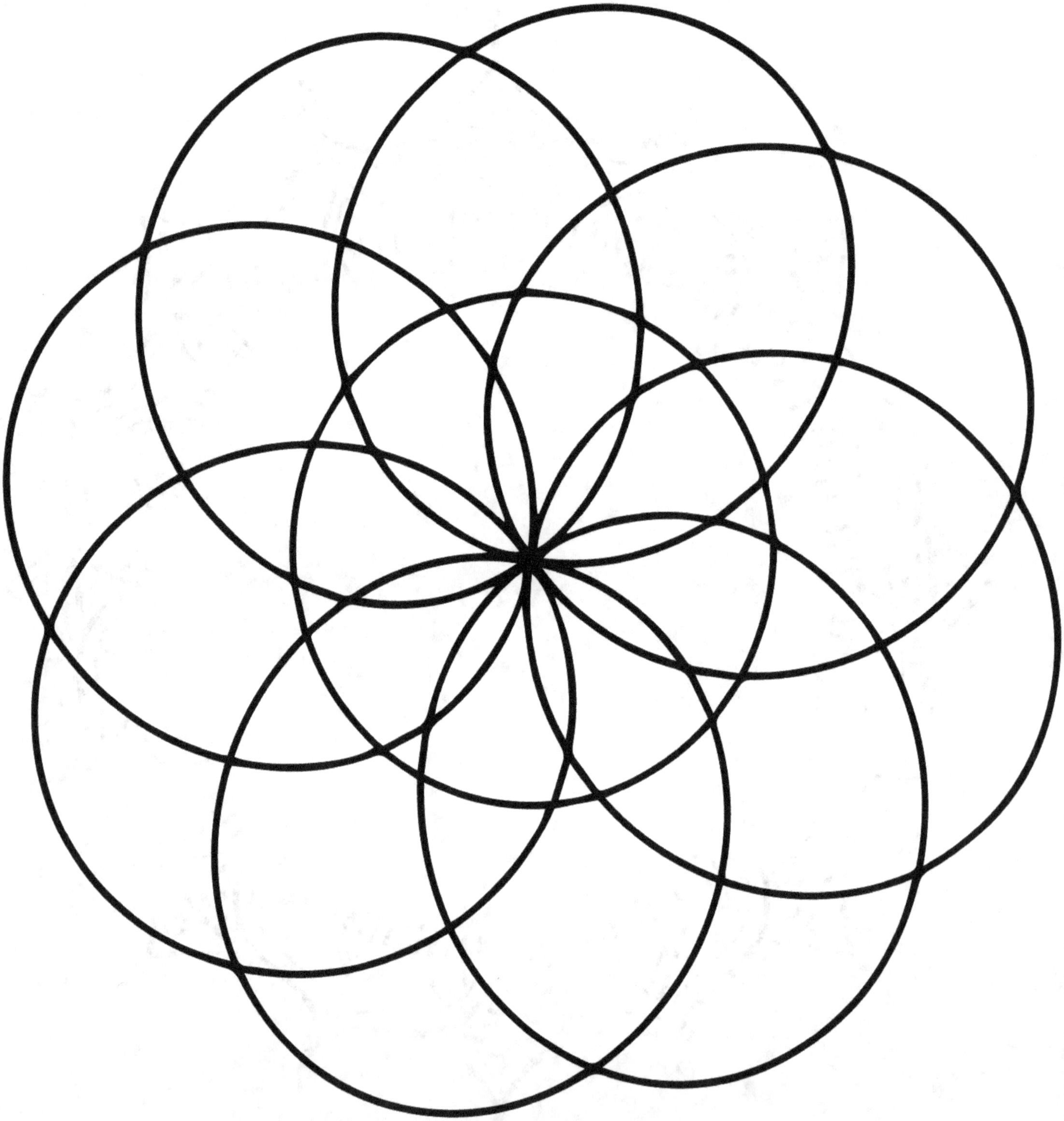

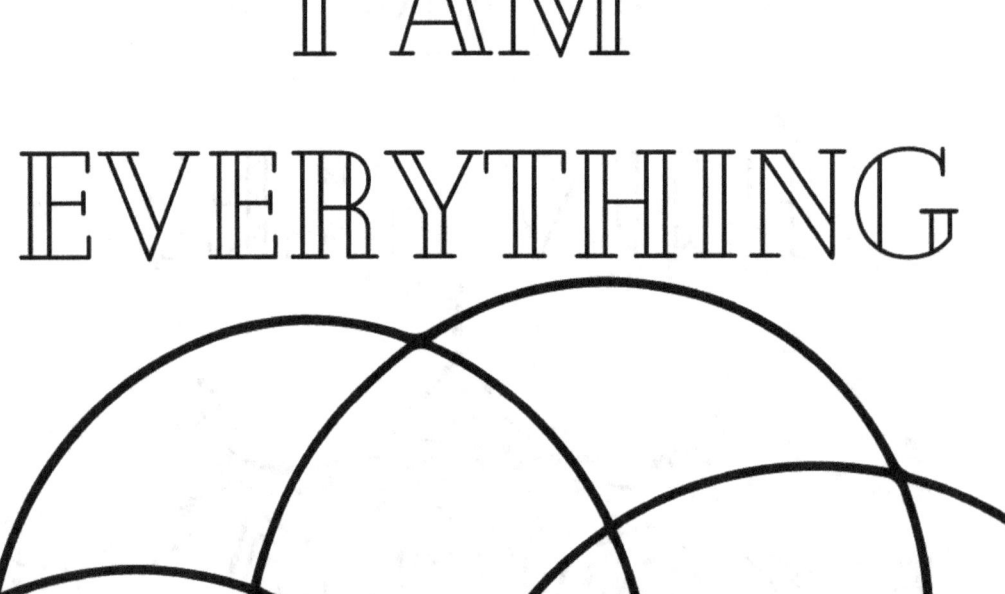

I AM A CHILD OF GOD

I WILL LEARN NEW SKILLS

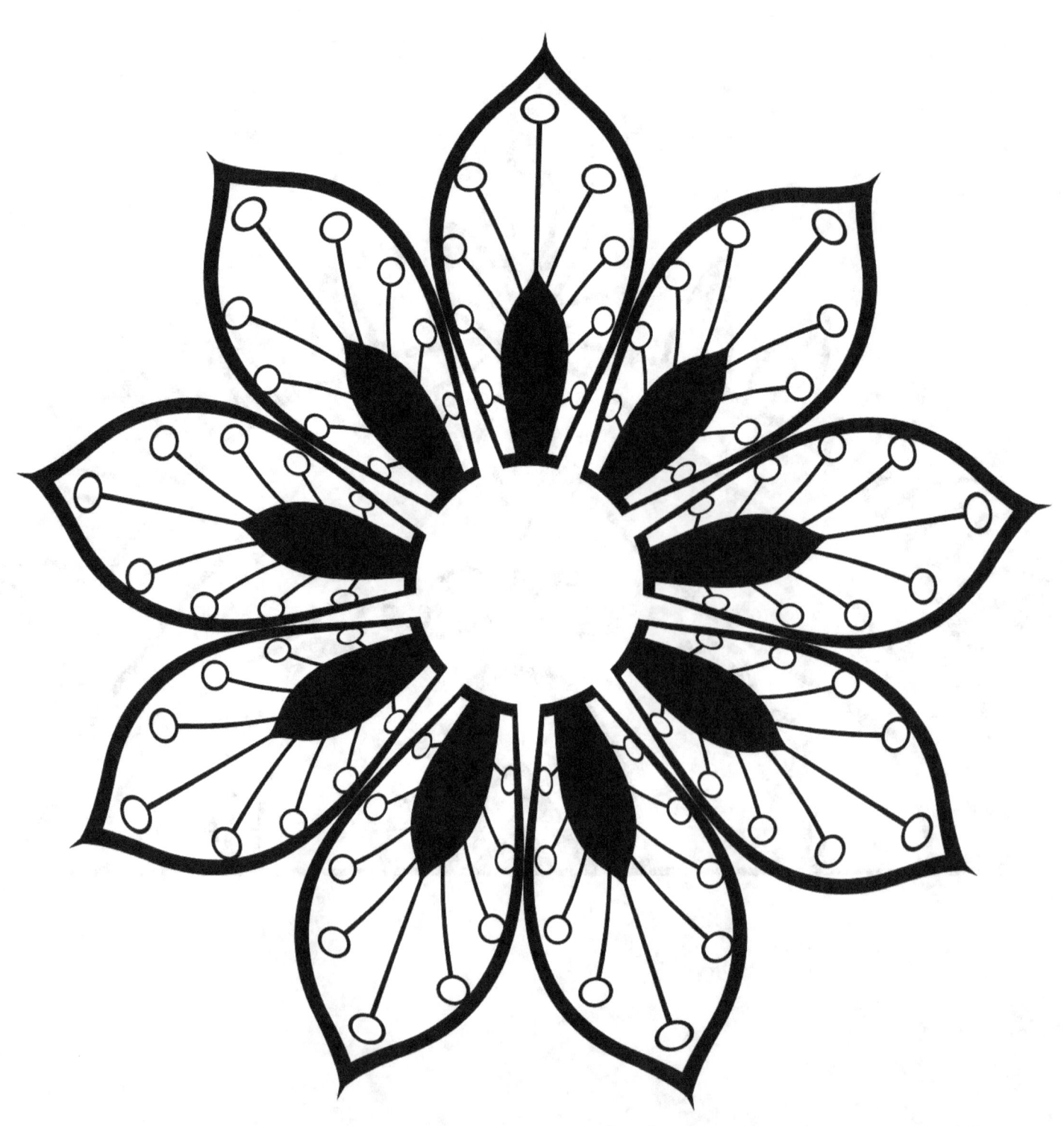

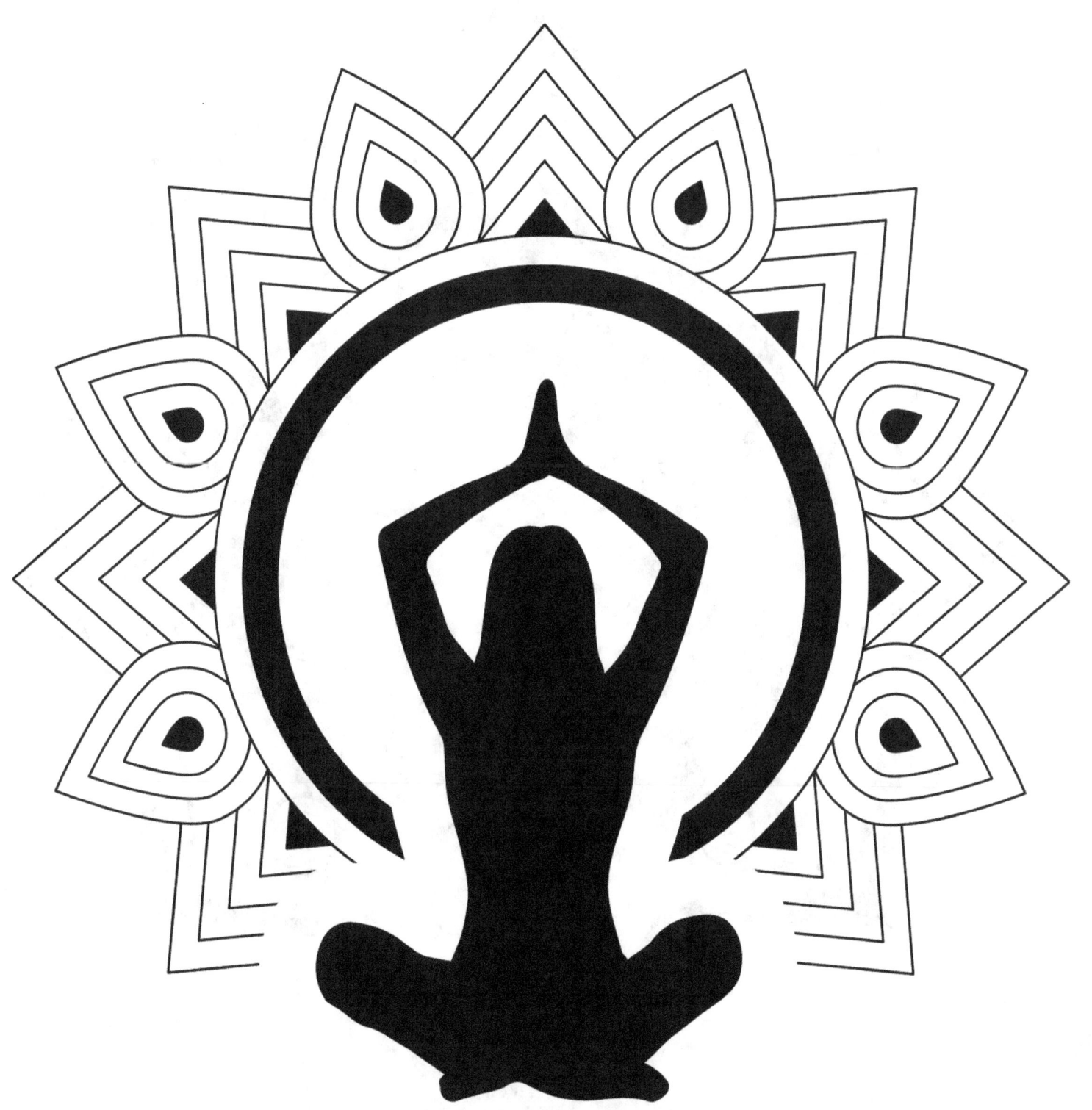

I AM SUCCESSFUL

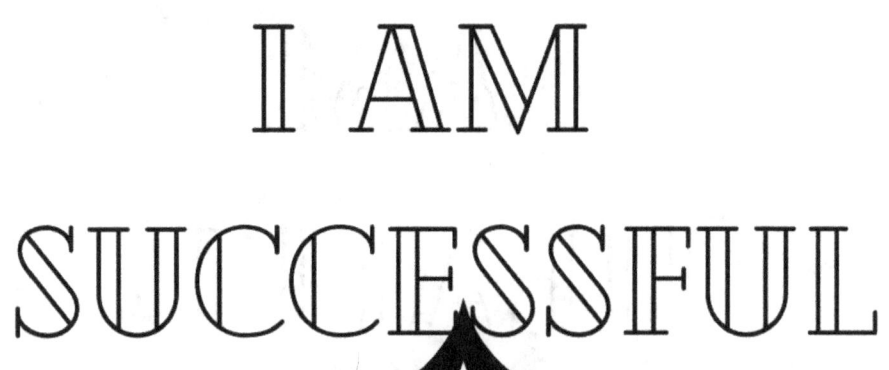

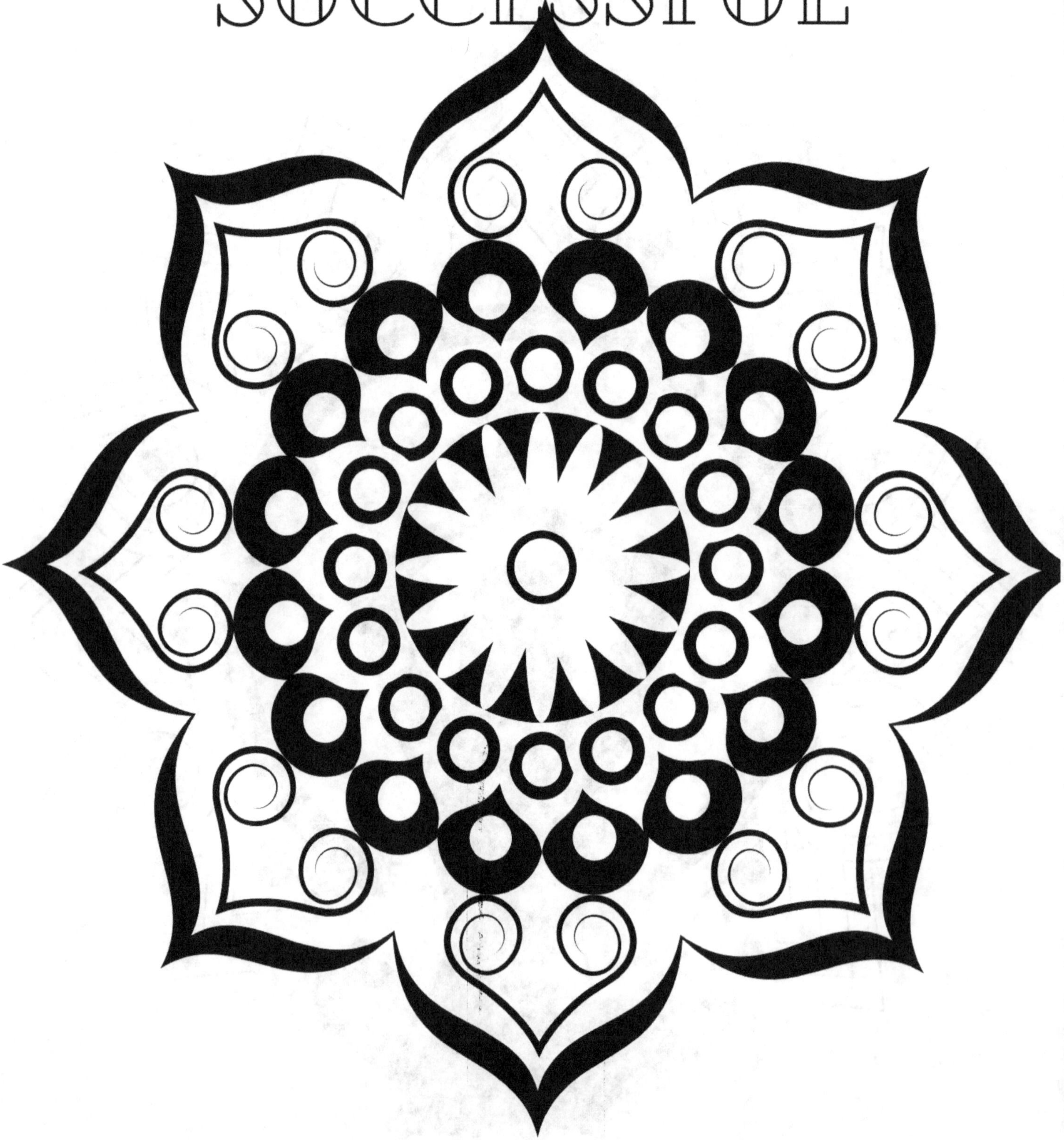

I AM UNSTOPPABLE

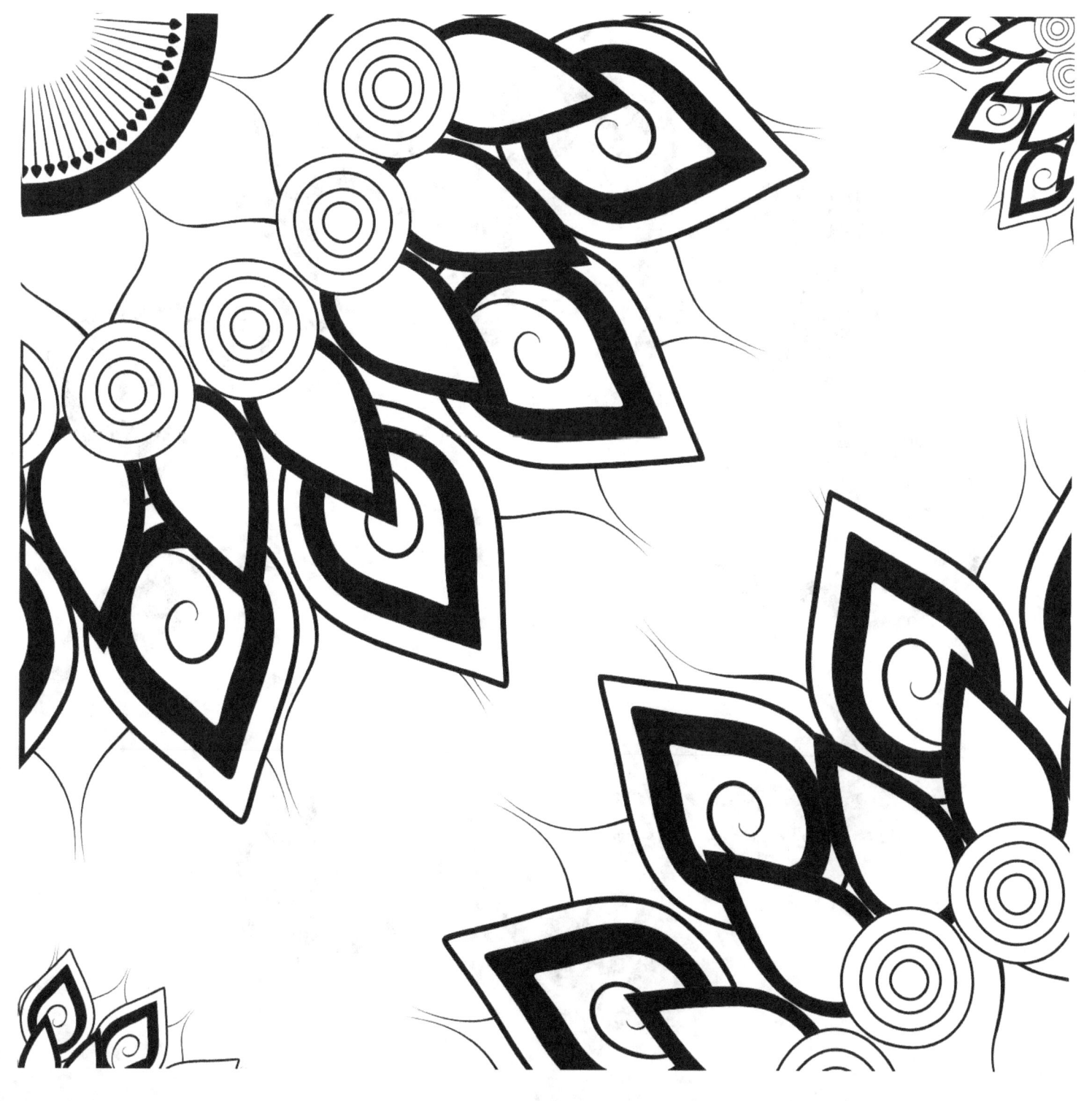

I AM DECISIVE

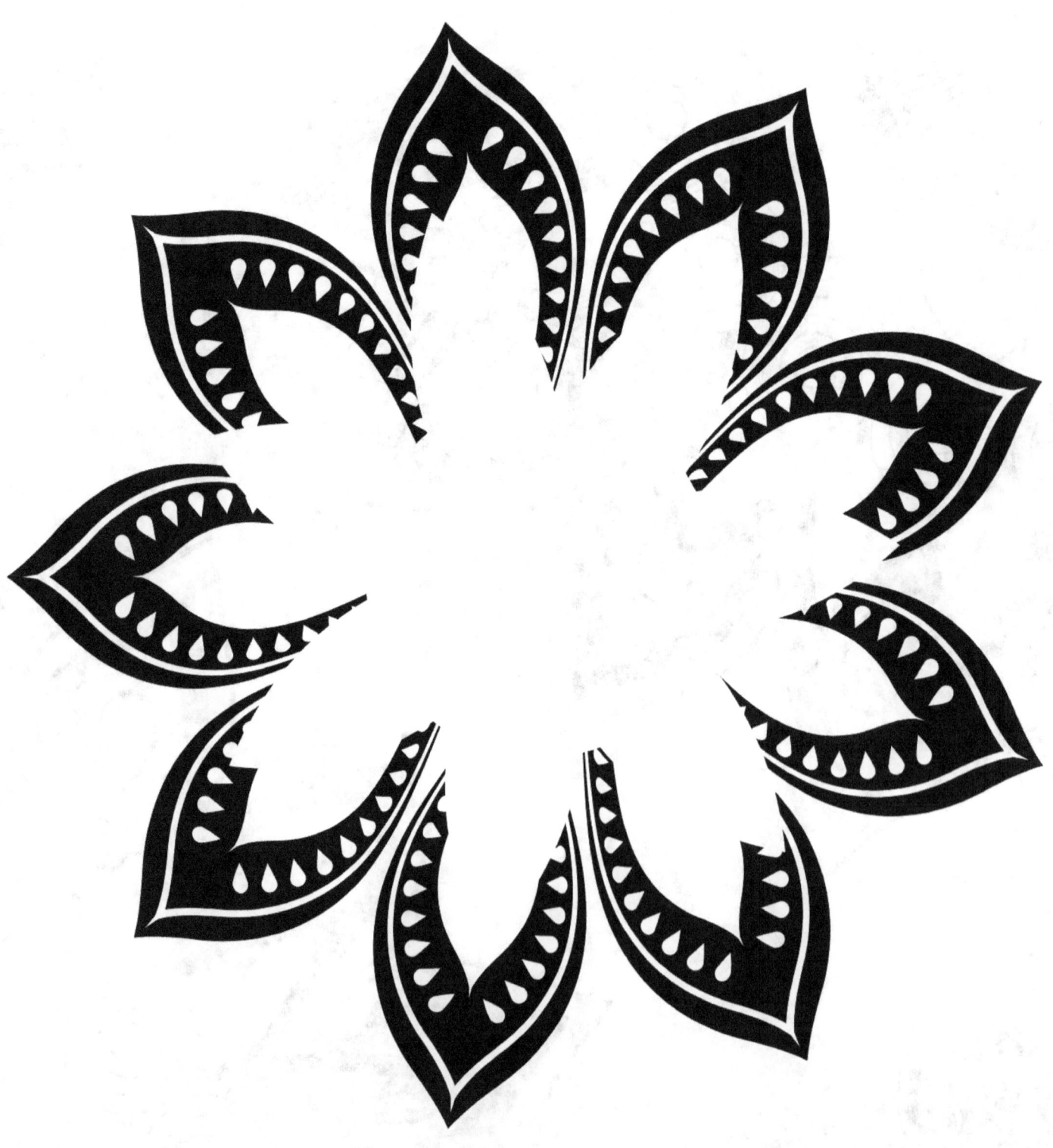

I FOLLOW MY DREAMS

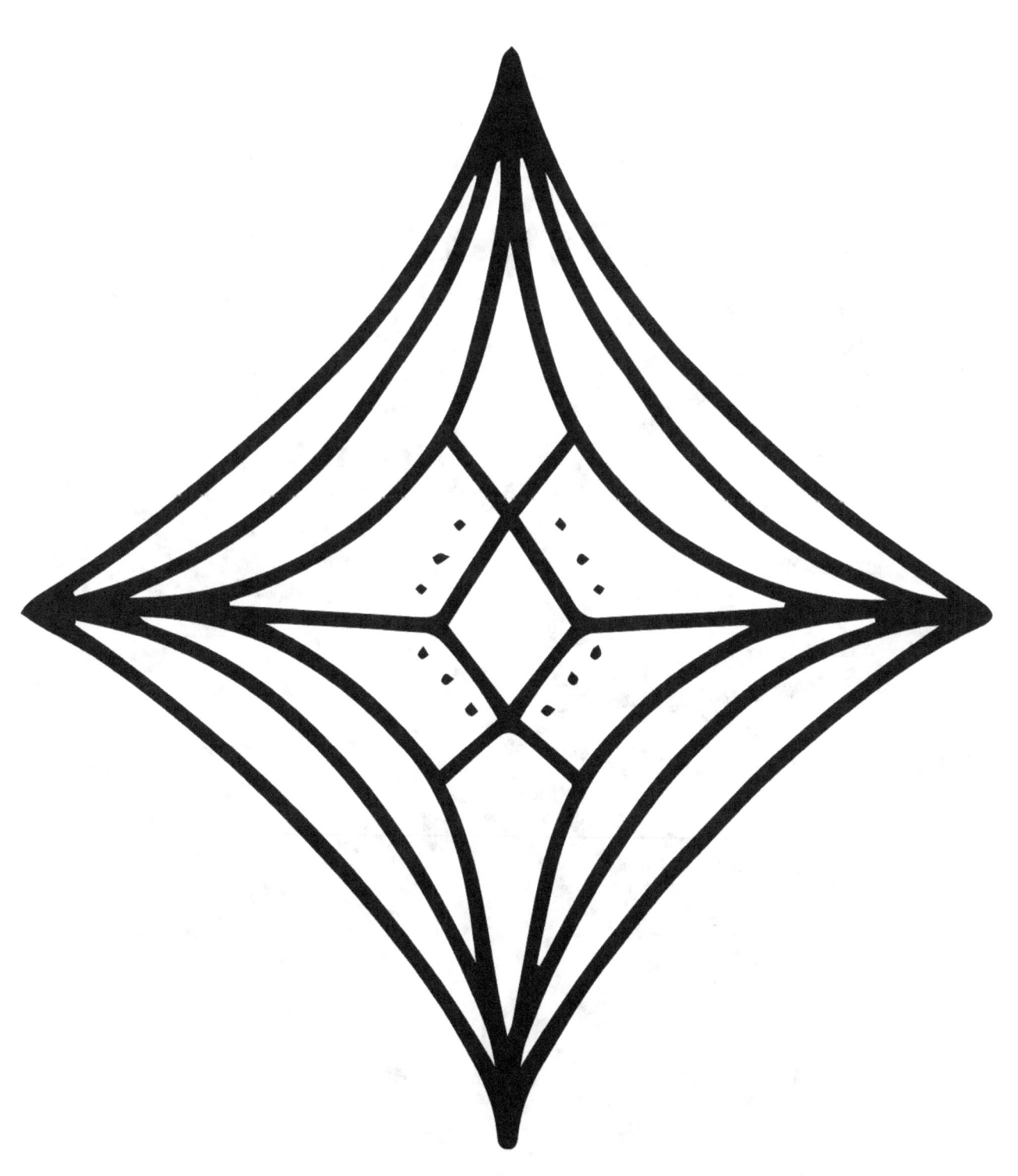

I AM THANKFUL

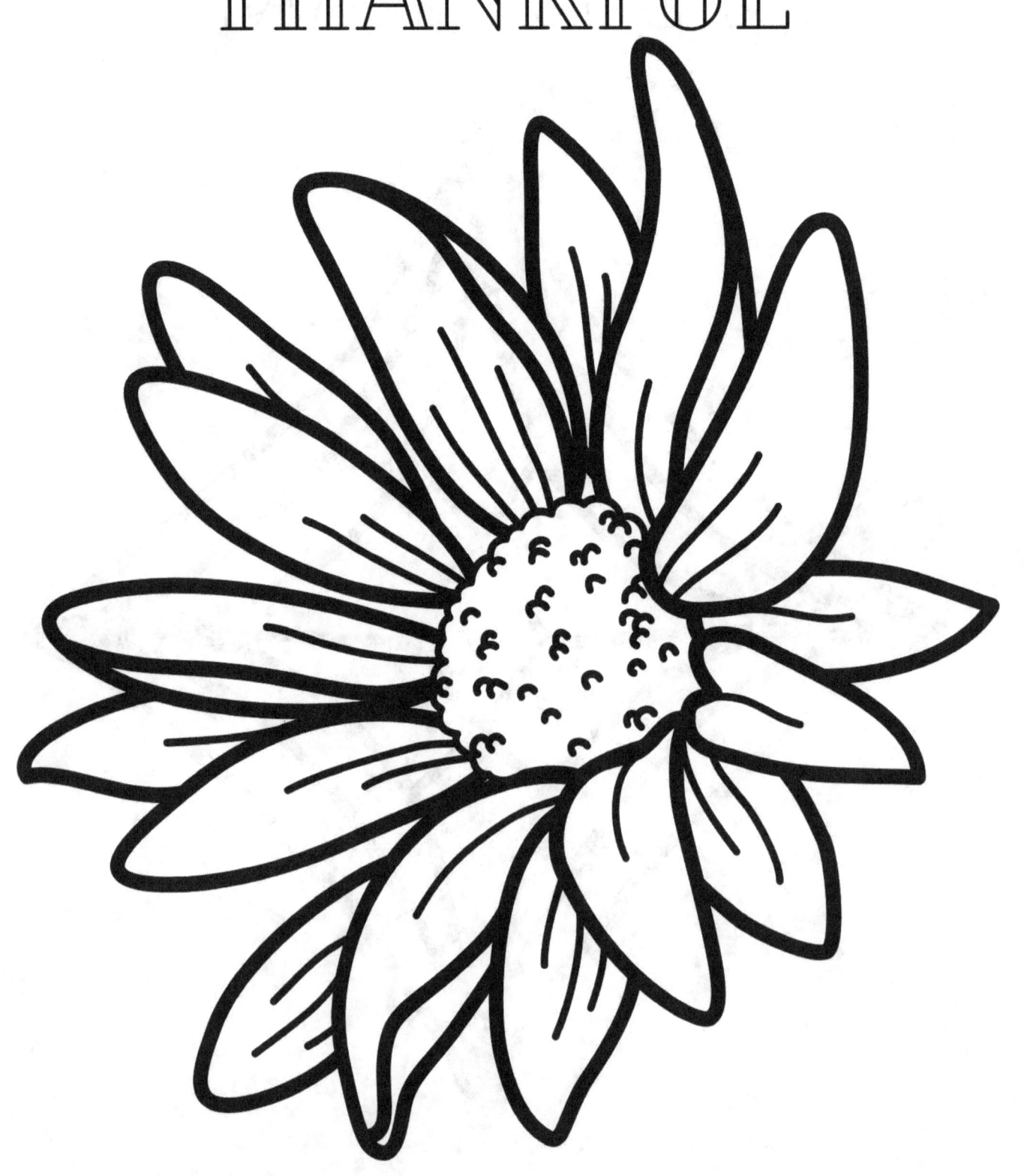

I UPLIFT OTHERS

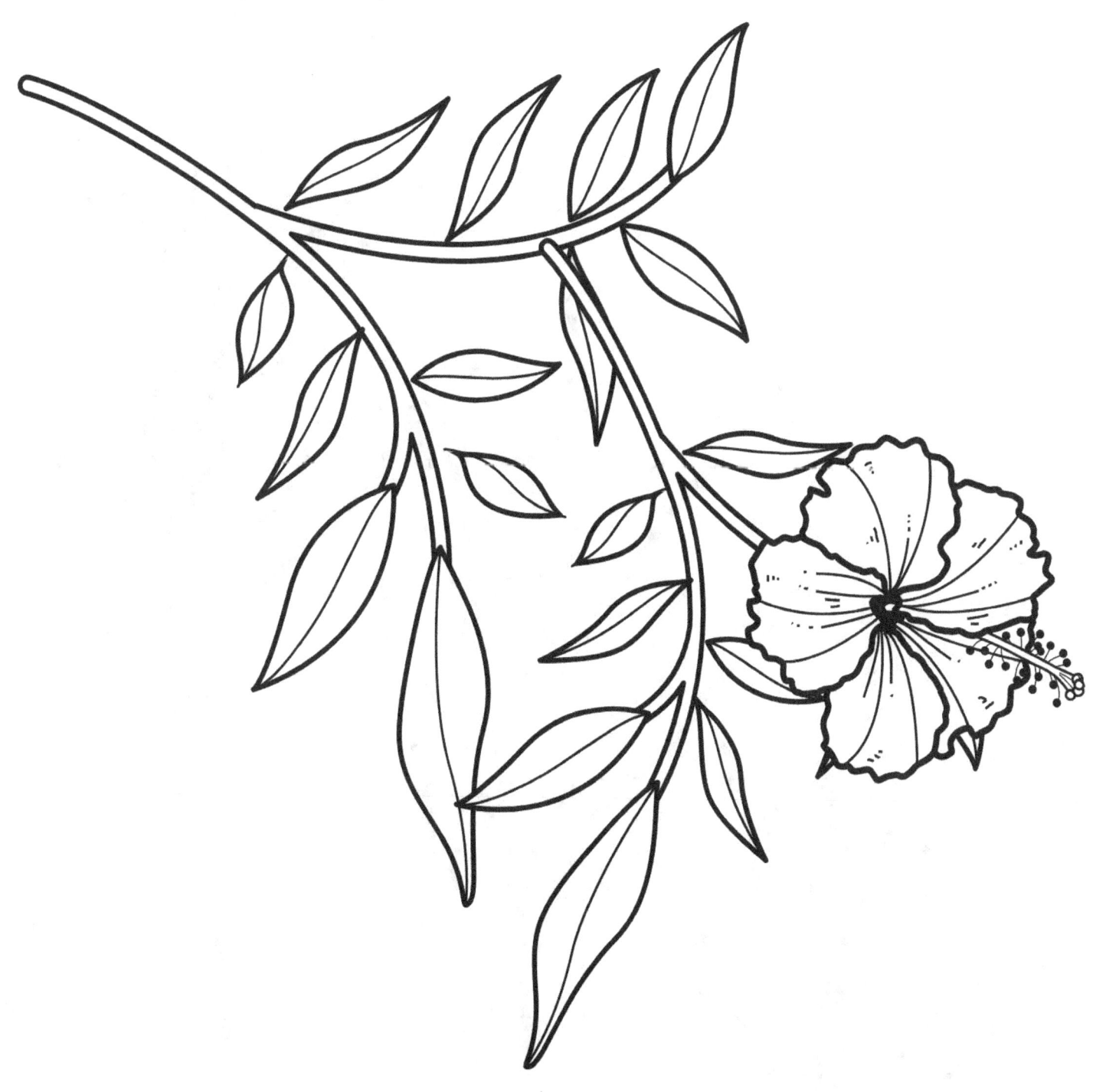

I AM PROGRESSING

KNOW YOUR WORTH

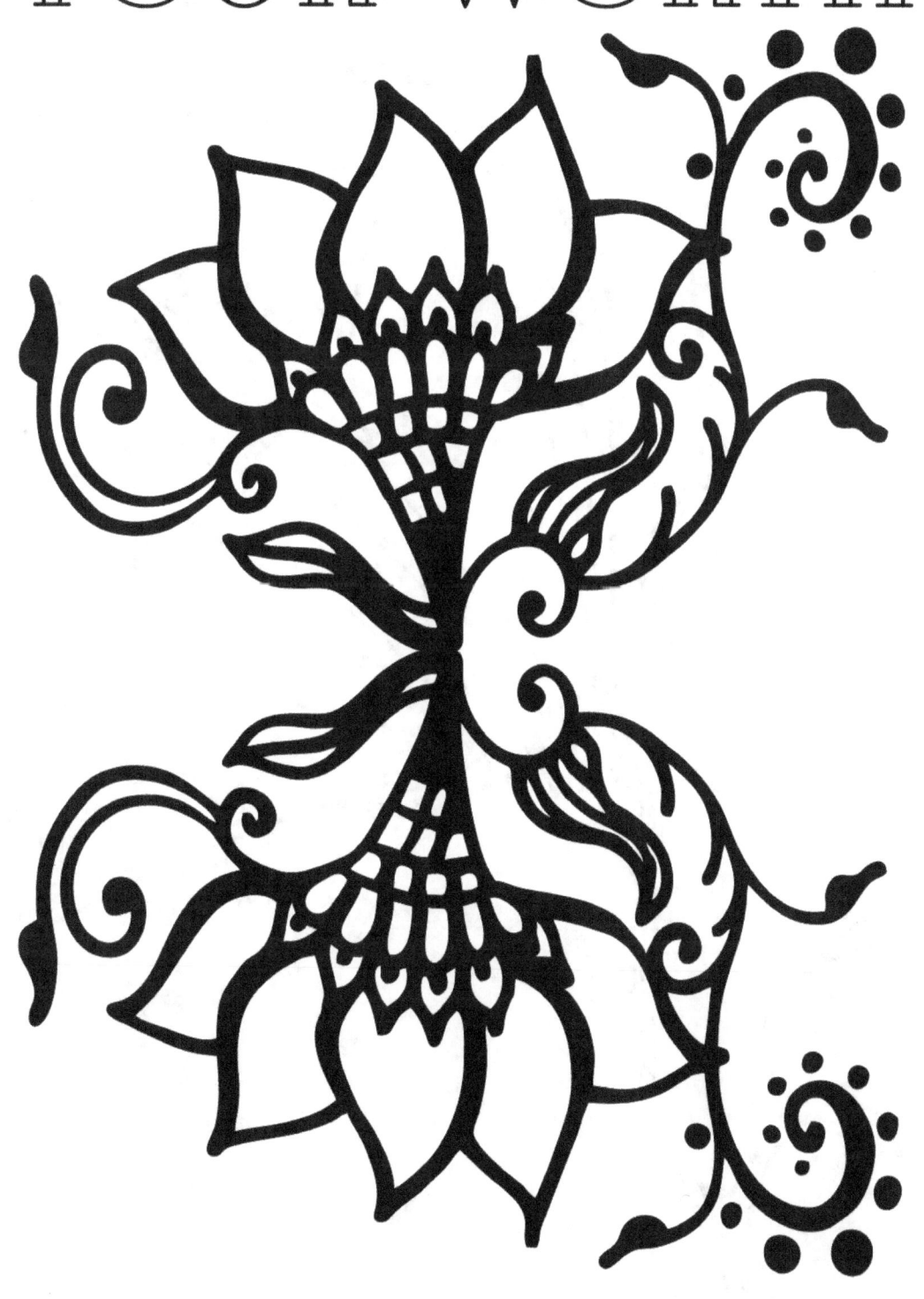

I HAVE GREAT IDEAS

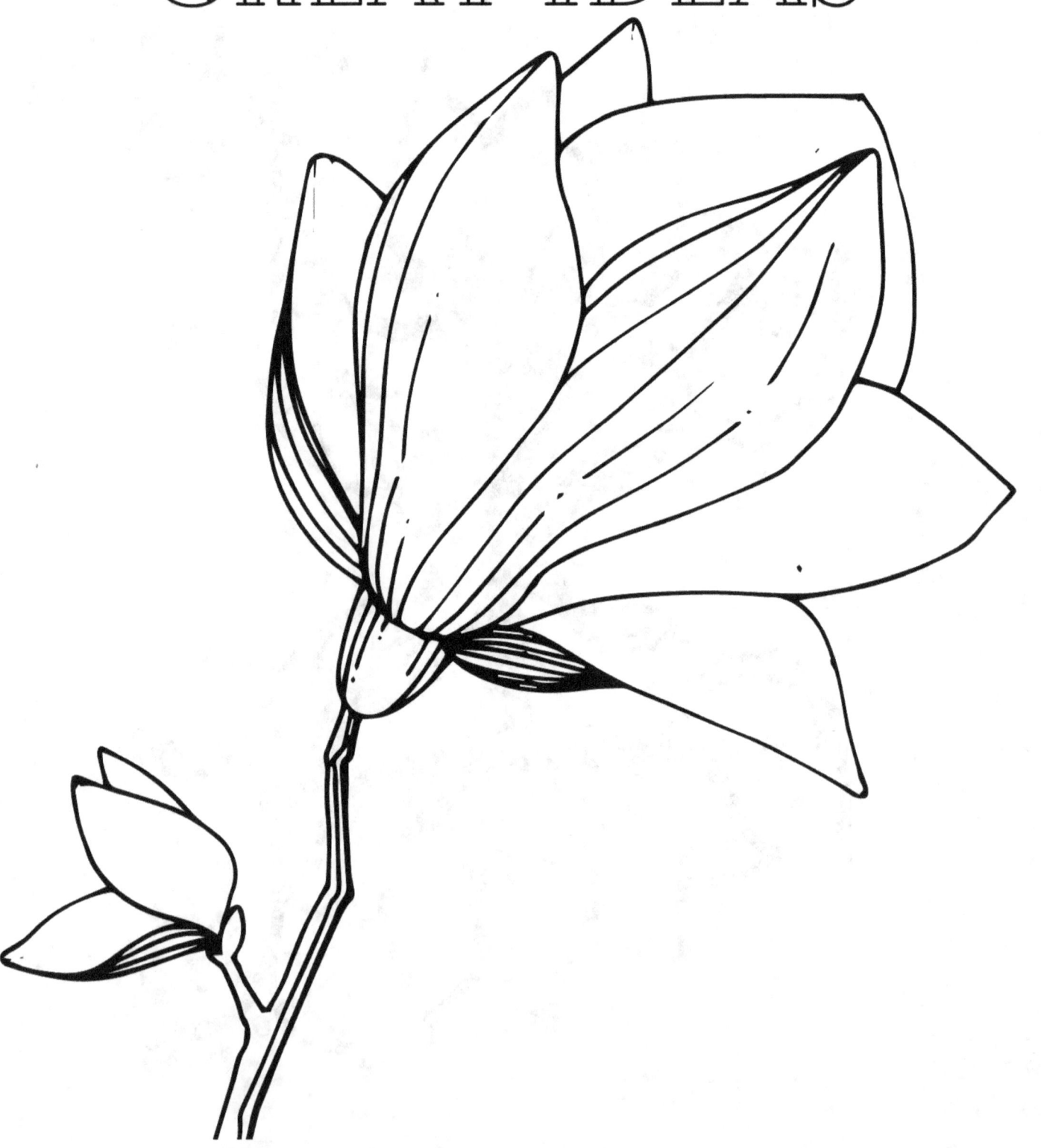

I WILL NOT OVERTHINK

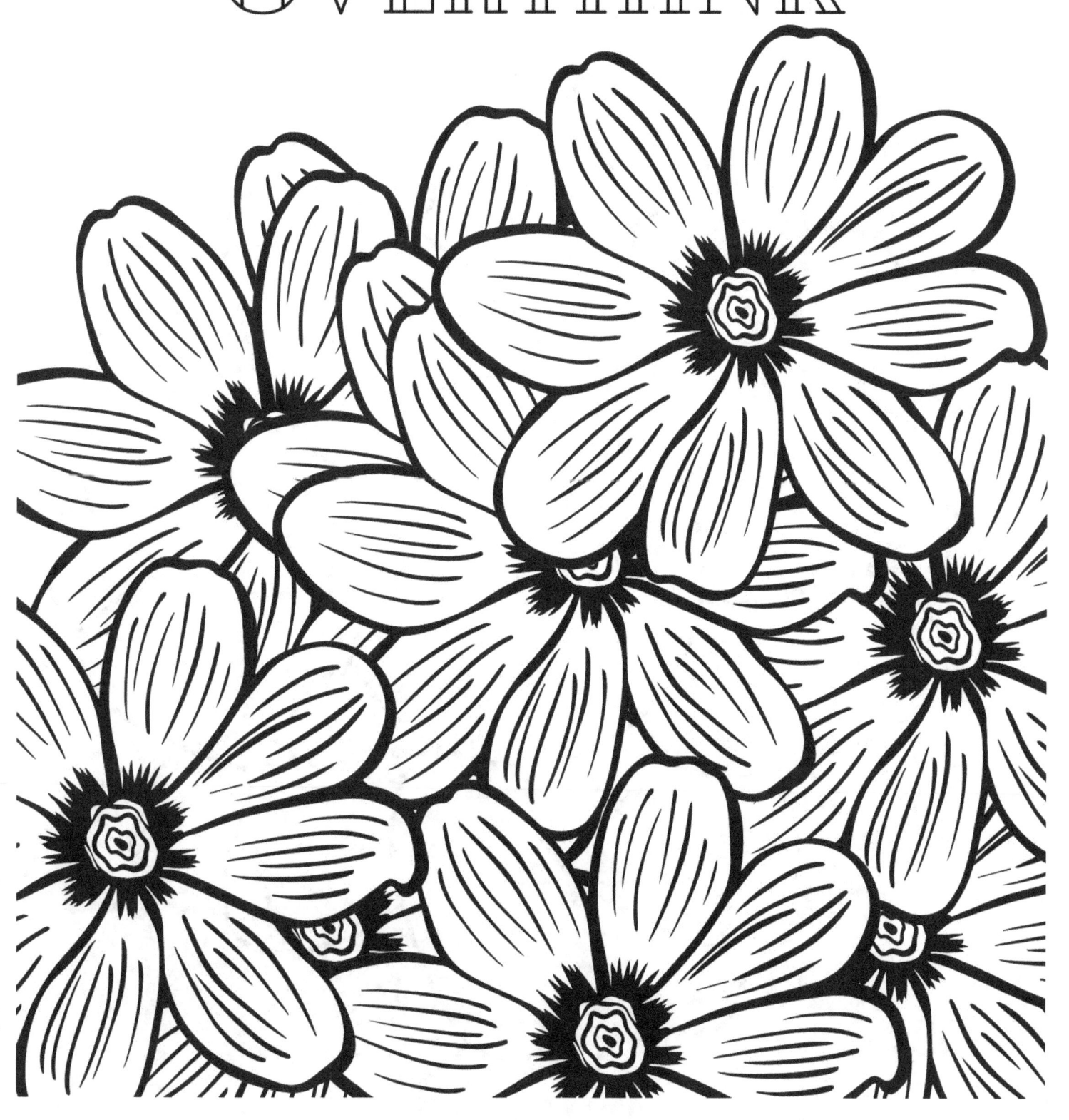

I MAKE TIME FOR MYSELF

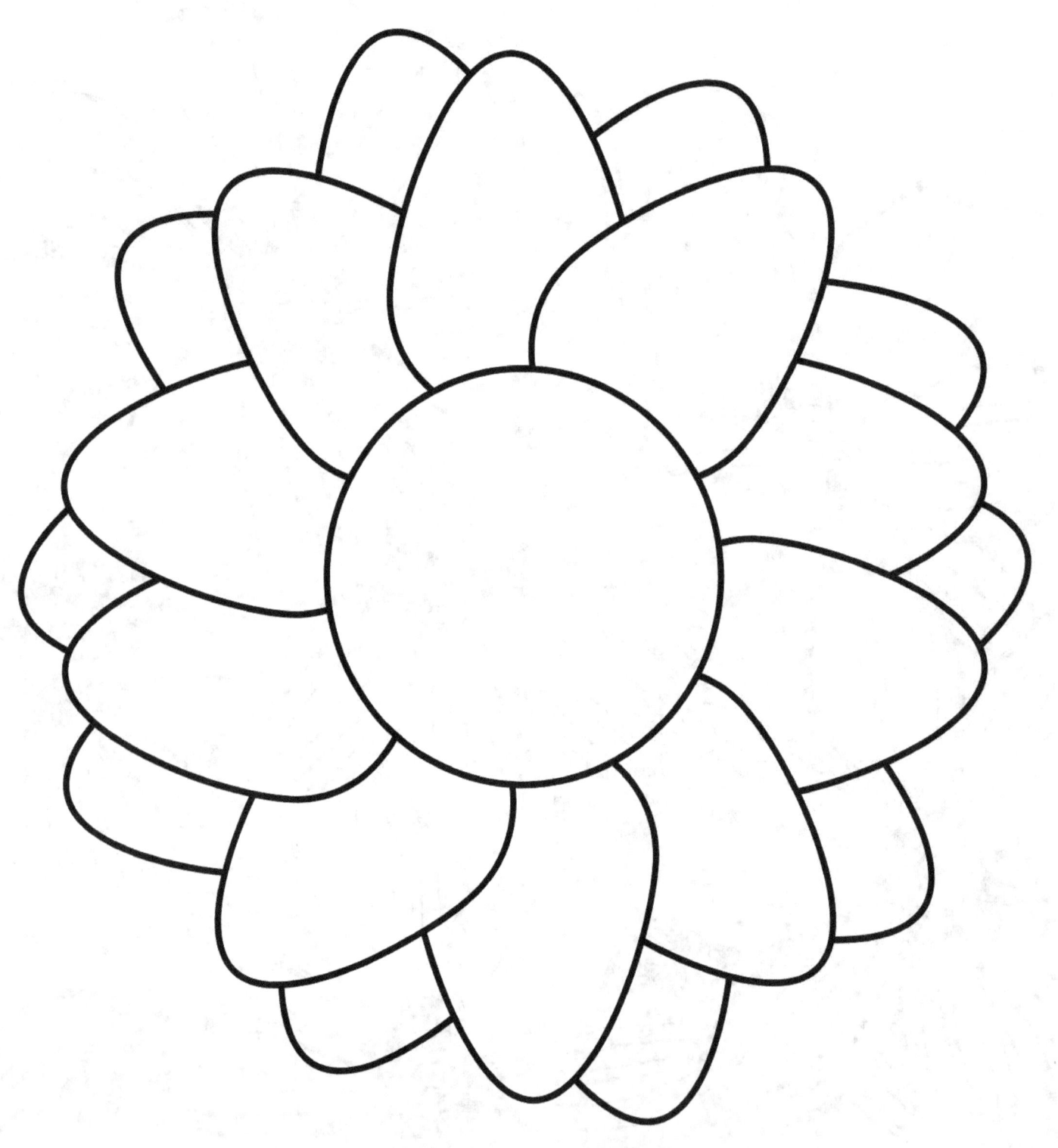

I AM ATTRACTIVE

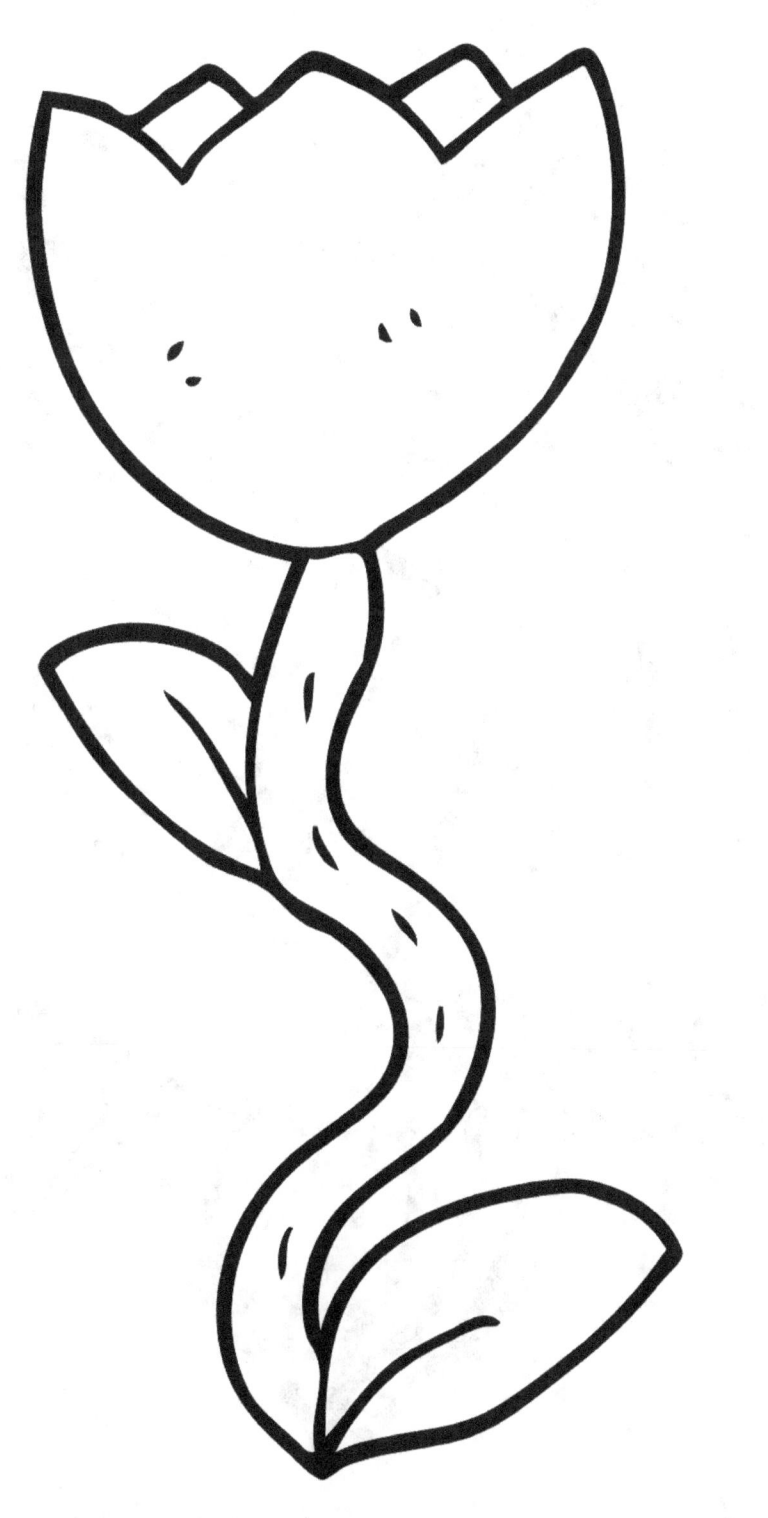

I CAN START OVER

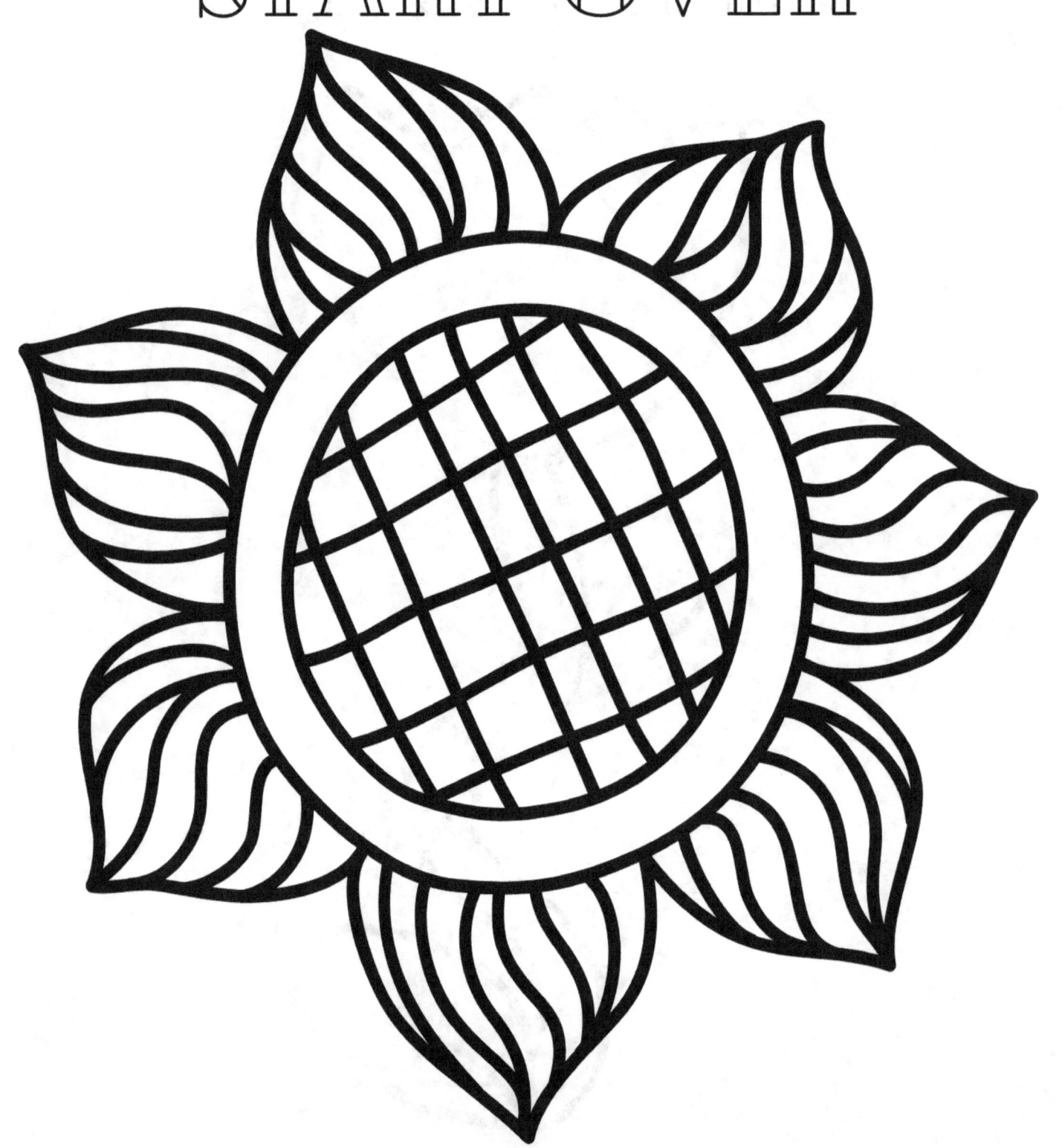

www.ingramcontent.com/pod-product-compliance
Lightning Source LLC
Chambersburg PA
CBHW081455220526
45466CB00008B/2655